아서,
도둑으로 몰리다!

CONTENTS

초보 영어 학습자라면 꼭 한번 읽어 봐야 할, 아서 챕터북 시리즈!

『아서 챕터북(Arthur Chapter Book)』 시리즈는 레이크우드(Lakewood) 초등학교에 다니는 주인공 아서(Arthur)가 일상에서 벌이는 다양한 에피소드를 담고 있습니다. 저자 마크 브라운(Marc Brown)이 미국 초등학생들을 위해 쓴 이 시리즈는, 누구나 공감할 만한 재미있는 스토리 덕분에 출간된 지 30년이 넘은 지금까지도 남녀노소 모두에게 큰 사랑을 받고 있습니다. 아서가 주인공으로 등장하는 이야기는 리더스북과 챕터북 등 다양한 형태로 출판되었으며, 미국에서만 누적 판매 부수 7천만 부를 돌파하고 TV 애니메이션으로 제작되는 등 높은 인기를 구가하고 있습니다.

특히 『아서 챕터북』 시리즈는 한국에서 초급 영어 학습자를 위한 최적의 원서로 큰 사랑을 받고 있기도 합니다. 많은 영어 교육 전문가들과 영어 학습법 도서에서 『아서 챕터북』 시리즈를 추천 도서로 소개하고 있으며, '엄마표·아빠표 영어'를 진행하는 부모님들에게도 반드시 거쳐 가야 하는 영어원서로 큰 지지를 얻고 있습니다.

번역과 단어장이 포함된 워크북, 그리고 오디오북까지 담긴 풀 패키지!

이 책은 영어원서 『아서 챕터북』 시리즈에, 탁월한 학습 효과를 거둘 수 있도록 다양한 콘텐츠를 덧붙인 책입니다.

- 영어원서: 본문에 나온 어려운 어휘에 볼드 처리가 되어 있어 단어를 더욱 분명하게 인지할 수 있고, 문맥에 따른 자연스러운 암기 효과를 얻을 수 있습니다.
- 단어장: 원서에 볼드 처리된 어휘의 의미가 완벽하게 정리되어 있어 사전 없이 원서를 수월하게 읽을 수 있으며, 반복해서 등장하는 단어에 '복습' 표기를 하여 자연스럽게 복습을 돕도록 구성했습니다.
- 번역: 영문과 비교할 수 있도록 직역에 가까운 번역을 담았습니다. 원서 읽기에 익숙하지 않은 초보 학습자도 어려움 없이 내용을 파악할 수 있습니다.
- 퀴즈: 챕터별로 내용을 확인하는 이해력 점검 퀴즈가 들어 있습니다.
- 오디오북: 미국 현지에서 판매 중인 빠른 속도의 오디오북(분당 약 145단어)과 국내에서 녹음된 따라 읽기용 오디오북(분당 약 110단어)을 기본으로 포함하고 있어, 듣기 훈련은 물론 소리 내어 읽기에까지 폭넓게 활용할 수 있습니다.

이 책의 수준과 타깃 독자

- 미국 원어민 기준: 유치원 ~ 초등학교 저학년
- 한국 학습자 기준: 초등학교 저학년 ~ 중학생
- 영어원서 완독 경험이 없는 초보 영어 학습자 (토익 기준 450~750점대)
- 도서 분량: 약 5,200단어
- 비슷한 수준의 다른 챕터북: Flat Stanley,★ The Zack Files,★ Tales from the Odyssey,★ Junie B. Jones,★ Magic Tree House, Marvin Redpost

  ★「롱테일 에디션」으로 출간된 도서

『아서 챕터북』 이렇게 읽어 보세요!

- **단어 암기는 이렇게!** 처음 리딩을 시작하기 전, 오늘 읽을 챕터에 나오는 단어들을 눈으로 쭉 훑어봅니다. 모르는 단어는 좀 더 주의 깊게 보되, 손으로 쓰면서 완벽하게 암기할 필요는 없습니다. 본문을 읽으면서 이 단어를 다시 만나게 되는데, 그 과정에서 단어의 쓰임새와 어감을 자연스럽게 익히게 됩니다. 이렇게 책을 읽은 후에 단어를 다시 한번 복습하세요. 복습할 때는 중요하다고 생각하는 단어들을 손으로 쓰면서 꼼꼼하게 외우는 것도 좋습니다. 이런 방식으로 책을 읽으면 많은 단어를 빠르고 부담 없이 익힐 수 있습니다.

- **리딩할 때는 리딩에만 집중하자!** 원서를 읽는 중간중간 모르는 단어가 나온다고 워크북을 바로 펼쳐 보거나, 곧바로 번역을 찾아보는 것은 크게 도움이 되지 않습니다. 모르는 단어나 이해되지 않는 문장들은 따로 가볍게 표시만 해 두고, 전체적인 맥락을 파악하며 속도감 있게 읽어 나가세요. 리딩을 할 때는 속도에 대한 긴장감을 잃지 않으면서 리딩에만 집중하는 것이 좋습니다. 모르는 단어와 문장은 리딩을 마친 후에 한꺼번에 정리하는 '리뷰' 시간을 통해 점검하는 시간을 가지면 됩니다. 리뷰를 할 때는 번역은 물론 단어장과 사전도 꼼꼼하게 확인하면서 어떤 이유에서 이해가 되지 않았는지 생각해 봅니다.

- **번역 활용은 이렇게!** 이해가 가지 않는 문장은 번역을 통해서 그 의미를 파악할 수 있습니다. 하지만 한국어와 영어는 정확히 1:1 대응이 되지 않기 때문에 번역을 활용하는 데에도 지혜가 필요합니다. 의역이 된 부분까지 억지로 의미

를 대응해서 이해하려고 하기보다, 어떻게 그런 의미가 만들어진 것인지 추측하면서 번역은 참고 자료로 활용하는 것이 좋습니다.

- **듣기 훈련은 이렇게!** 리스닝 실력을 향상시키고 싶다면 오디오북을 적극적으로 활용해 보세요. 처음에는 오디오북을 틀어 놓고 눈으로 해당 내용을 따라 읽으면서 훈련을 하고, 이것이 익숙해지면 오디오북만 틀어 놓고 '귀를 통해' 책을 읽어 보세요. 눈으로 읽지 않은 책이라도 귀를 통해 이해할 수 있을 정도가 되면, 이후에 영어 듣기로 어려움을 겪는 일은 거의 없을 것입니다.

- **소리 내어 읽고 녹음하자!** 이 책은 특히 소리 내어 읽기(voice reading)에 최적화된 문장 길이와 구조를 가지고 있습니다. 오디오북 기본 구성에 포함된 '따라 읽기용' 오디오북을 활용해 소리 내어 읽기 훈련을 시작해 보세요! 내가 읽은 것을 녹음하고 들어보는 과정을 통해 자연스럽게 어휘와 표현을 복습하고, 의식적·무의식적으로 발음을 교정하게 됩니다. 이렇게 영어로 소리를 만들어 본 경험은 이후 탄탄한 스피킹 실력의 밑거름이 될 것입니다.

- **2~3번 반복해서 읽자!** 영어 초보자라면 처음부터 완벽하게 이해하려고 하는 것보다는 2~3회 반복해서 읽을 것을 추천합니다. 처음 원서를 읽을 때는 생소한 단어들과 스토리 때문에 내용 파악에 급급할 수밖에 없습니다. 하지만 일단 내용을 파악한 후에 다시 읽으면 문장 구조나 어휘의 활용에 더 집중하게 되고, 원서를 더 깊이 있게 읽을 수 있습니다. 그 과정에서 리딩 속도에 탄력이 붙고 리딩 실력 또한 더 확고히 다지게 됩니다.

- **'시리즈'로 꾸준히 읽자!** 한 작가의 책을 시리즈로 읽는 것 또한 영어 실력 향상에 큰 도움이 됩니다. 같은 등장인물이 다시 나오기 때문에 내용 파악이 더 수월할 뿐 아니라, 작가가 사용하는 어휘와 표현들도 반복되기 때문에 탁월한 복습 효과까지 얻을 수 있습니다. 롱테일북스의 『아서 챕터북』 시리즈는 현재 10권, 총 50,000단어 분량이 출간되어 있습니다. 시리즈를 꾸준히 읽다 보면 영어 실력이 자연스럽게 향상될 것입니다.

원서 본문 구성

내용이 담긴 원서 본문입니다.

원어민이 읽는 일반 원서와 같은 텍스트지만, 암기해야 할 중요 어휘들은 볼드체로 표시되어 있습니다. 이 어휘들은 지금 들고 계신 워크북에 챕터별로 정리되어 있습니다.

학습 심리학 연구 결과에 따르면, 한 단어씩 따로 외우는 단어 암기는 거의 효과가 없다고 합니다. 단어를 제대로 외우기 위해서는 문맥(context) 속에서 단어를 암기해야 하며, 한 단어당 문맥 속에서 15번 이상 마주칠 때 완벽하게 암기할 수 있다고 합니다.

이 책의 본문에서는 중요 어휘를 볼드체로 강조하여, 문맥 속의 단어들을 더 확실히 인지(word cognition in context)하도록 돕고 있습니다. 또한 대부분의 중요 단어들은 다른 챕터에서도 반복해서 등장하기 때문에 이 책을 읽는 것만으로도 자연스럽게 어휘력을 향상시킬 수 있습니다.

본문 하단에는 내용 이해를 돕기 위한 '각주'가 첨가되어 있습니다. 각주는 굳이 암기할 필요는 없지만, 알아 두면 도움이 될 만한 정보를 설명하고 있습니다. 각주를 참고하면 스토리를 더 깊이 있게 이해할 수 있어 원서를 읽는 재미가 배가됩니다.

워크북(Workbook) 구성

Check Your Reading Speed

해당 챕터의 단어 수가 기록되어 있어, 리딩 속도를 측정할 수 있습니다. 특히 리딩 속도를 중시하는 독자들이 유용하게 사용할 수 있습니다.

Build Your Vocabulary

본문에 볼드 표시되어 있는 단어들이 정리되어 있습니다. 리딩 전·후에 반복해서 보면 원서를 더욱 쉽게 읽을 수 있고, 어휘력도 빠르게 향상될 것입니다.

단어는 〈스펠링 – 빈도 – 발음기호 – 품사 – 한글 뜻 – 영문 뜻〉 순서로 표기되어 있으며 빈도 표시(★)가 많을수록 필수 어휘입니다. 반복해서 등장하는 단어는 빈도 대신 '복습'으로 표기되어 있습니다. 품사는 아래와 같이 표기했습니다.

n. 명사 ｜ a. 형용사 ｜ ad. 부사 ｜ v. 동사

conj. 접속사 ｜ prep. 전치사 ｜ int. 감탄사 ｜ idiom 숙어 및 관용구

Comprehension Quiz

간단한 퀴즈를 통해 읽은 내용에 대한 이해력을 점검해 볼 수 있습니다.

한국어 번역

영문과 비교할 수 있도록 최대한 직역에 가까운 번역을 담았습니다.

오디오북 구성

이 책에는 '듣기 훈련'과 '소리 내어 읽기 훈련'을 위한 2가지 종류의 오디오북이 기본으로 포함되어 있습니다.

- 듣기 훈련용 오디오북: 분당 145단어 속도 (미국 현지에서 판매 중인 오디오북)
- 따라 읽기용 오디오북: 분당 110단어 속도 (소리 내어 읽기 훈련용 오디오북)

 QR 코드를 인식하여 따라 읽기용 & 듣기 훈련용 두 가지 오디오북을 들어보세요! 더불어 롱테일북스 홈페이지 (www.longtailbooks.co.kr)에서도 오디오북 MP3 파일을 다운로드 받을 수 있습니다.

Chapter 1

1. Who was the narrator of the story?

　A. Mrs. MacGrady

　B. Buster

　C. Binky

　D. Arthur

2. How was Arthur helping the fire department?

　A. He was collecting money for the fire department to buy a puppy.

　B. He was collecting money for the fire department to buy a pony.

　C. He was collecting money for the fire department to buy a kitten.

　D. He was collecting money for the fire department to buy brownies.

3. **What did Binky tell Arthur to do after giving him a quarter?**

A. He told him to tell other people that he hated puppies.

B. He told him to tell other people that he stole a quarter.

C. He told him not to tell anyone he gave a quarter.

D. He told him not to tell anyone he liked puppies.

4. **Why was Buster wearing a hat?**

A. It was a gift from Arthur.

B. It was part of his detective kit.

C. It was part of his school play costume.

D. It was part of his homework assignment.

5. **What was the secret information that Buster found?**

A. There was a free brownie for students at the picnic.

B. There was a fourth-grade picnic on Friday.

C. There was a fund drive for a puppy.

D. There was a third-grade picnic on Friday.

1분에 몇 단어를 읽는지 리딩 속도를 측정해보세요.

$$\frac{514 \ words}{reading \ time \ (\qquad) \ sec} \times 60 = (\qquad) \ WPM$$

Build Your Vocabulary

private [práivət] a. 사적인, 개인적인
Your private things belong only to you, or may only be used by you.

case [keis] n. 사건, 경우, 사례
A case is a crime or mystery that the police are investigating.

involve [inválv] v. 포함하다; (상황·사건·활동이 사람을) 관련시키다
If a situation or activity involves something, that thing is a necessary part or consequence of it.

pal [pæl] n. 친구, 동료; vi. 친구가 되다
Your pals are your friends.

missing [mísiŋ] a. (제자리나 집에 있지 않고) 없어진; 빠진, 누락된
If something is missing, it is not in its usual place, and you cannot find it.

quarter [kwɔ́:rtər] n. 25센트; 4분의 1; 15분
A quarter is an American or Canadian coin that is worth 25 cents.

ordinary [ɔ́:rdənèri] a. 보통의, 평범한
Ordinary people or things are normal and not special or different in any way.

hallway [hɔ́:lwèi] n. 복도, 통로; 현관
A hallway in a building is a long passage with doors into rooms on both sides of it.

bowl [boul] n. 사발, 그릇
A bowl is a round container with a wide uncovered top.

fire department [fáiər dipá:rtmənt] n. 소방서, 소방국
The fire department is an organization which has the job of putting out fires.

puppy [pápi] n. 강아지
A puppy is a young dog.

block [blak] vt. (길 등을) 막다, 방해하다; n. 덩어리, 블록
To block a road, channel, or pipe means to put an object across it or in it so that nothing can pass through it or along it.

hall [hɔːl] n. (건물의) 복도, 통로; (건물 입구 안쪽의) 현관; 넓은 방[건물]
A hall in a building is a long passage with doors into rooms on both sides of it.

collect [kəlékt] v. 모금하다; 모으다, 수집하다
If you collect for a charity or for a present for someone, you ask people to give you money for it.

fund [fʌnd] n. (특정 목적을 위한) 기금, 자금; v. 자금을 제공하다
Funds are amounts of money that are available to be spent, especially money that is given to an organization or person for a particular purpose.

drive [draiv] n. (조직적인) 모금 운동; 드라이브, 자동차 여행; v. (차를) 몰다, 운전하다
A drive is a special effort made by a group of people for a particular purpose.

spot [spat] n. 반점, 얼룩; 장소, 지점; vt. 발견하다, 분별하다
Spots are small, round, colored areas on a surface.

consider [kənsídər] v. 고려하다, 숙고하다
If you consider something, you think about it carefully.

weigh [wei] vt. (결정을 내리기 전에) 따져 보다, 저울질하다; 무게[체중]를 달다
If you weigh the facts about a situation, you consider them very carefully before you make a decision, especially by comparing the various facts involved.

shiny [ʃáini] a. 빛나는, 반짝거리는
Shiny things are bright and reflect light.

roll [roul] v. 구르다, 굴러가다[오다]; 굴리다; n. 굴리기, 던지기; 통, 두루마리
When something rolls or when you roll it, it moves along a surface, turning over many times.

snuffle [snʌfl] v. 코를 훌쩍이다, 코를 킁킁거리다; n. 코를 킁킁거리는 소리
If a person or an animal snuffles, they breathe in noisily through their nose, for example because they have a cold.

wag [wæg] v. (꼬리 등을) 흔들다, 계속 움직이다; n. 흔들기
When a dog wags its tail, it repeatedly waves its tail from side to side.

flip [flip] v. 톡 던지다; 홱 뒤집(히)다; (책장을) 휙휙 넘기다; n. 톡 던지기; 공중제비
If you flip something, especially a coin, you use your thumb to make it turn over and over, as it goes through the air.

glare [glɛər] v. 노려보다, 쏘아보다; n. 노려봄
If you glare at someone, you look at them with an angry expression on your face.

satisfy [sǽtisfài] v. 만족시키다; 채우다 (satisfied a. 만족한, 흡족한)
If someone or something satisfies you, they give you enough of what you want or need to make you pleased or contented.

yell [jel] v. 소리치다, 고함치다; n. 고함소리, 부르짖음
If you yell, you shout loudly, usually because you are excited, angry, or in pain.

goofy [gúːfi] a. 바보 같은, 얼빠진
If you describe someone or something as goofy, you think they are rather silly or ridiculous.

* **detective** [ditéktiv] n. 탐정, 형사
A detective is someone whose job is to discover what has happened in a crime or other situation and to find the people involved.

* **kit** [kit] n. (도구·장비) 세트, (특정 활동용) 복장
Kit is special clothing and equipment that you use when you take part in a particular activity, especially a sport.

snoop [snu:p] v. 염탐하다, 기웃거리다; n. 염탐
If someone snoops around a place, they secretly look around it in order to find out things.

* **crime** [kraim] n. 범행, 범죄
A crime is an illegal action or activity for which a person can be punished by law.

* **brim** [brim] n. (모자의) 챙; v. (넘칠 듯) 그득하다; 가득 채우다
The brim of a hat is the wide part that sticks outward at the bottom.

* **peer** [piər] vi. 눈여겨보다, 응시하다
If you peer at something, you look at it very hard, usually because it is difficult to see clearly.

go no further idiom (비밀이 다른 사람에게로) 새어나가지 않다
If you tell someone that a secret will go no further, you promise not to tell it to anyone else.

* **nod** [nad] v. (고개를) 끄덕이다, 끄덕여 나타내다; n. (고개를) 끄덕임
If you nod, you move your head downward and upward to show agreement, understanding, or approval.

* **lean** [li:n] v. 기울다, (몸을) 숙이다
When you lean in a particular direction, you bend your body in that direction.

* **forward** [fɔ́:rwərd] ad. (위치가) 앞으로; (시간상으로) 미래로
If you move or look forward, you move or look in a direction that is in front of you.

whisper [hwíspər] v. 속삭이다; n. 속삭임
When you whisper, you say something very quietly.

roll one's eyes idiom 눈을 굴리다
If you roll your eyes, you show with your eyes that you don't believe someone or aren't interested in what they're saying.

sign [sain] n. 표지판, 표시; 징후, 흔적; v. 서명하다; 신호를 보내다
Signs give you information about something, or give you a warning or an instruction.

give up idiom 포기하다, 단념하다
If you give up, you decide that you cannot do something and stop trying to do it.

arcade [a:rkéid] n. 오락실, 게임 센터
An arcade is a commercial establishment featuring rows of coin-operated games.

figure [fígjər] v. 생각하다, 판단하다; 계산하다; n. 형태, 형상; 수치, 숫자
If you figure that something is the case, you think or guess that it is the case.

probably [prábəbli] ad. 아마
If you say that something is probably the case, you think that it is likely to be the case, although you are not sure.

empty [émpti] vt. 비우다; a. 빈, 공허한
If you empty a container, or empty something out of it, you remove its contents, especially by tipping it up.

Chapter 2

1. **Where did Arthur go to see Mrs. MacGrady?**
   A. The cafeteria kitchen
   B. The janitor's closet
   C. The principal's office
   D. The teacher's lounge

2. **What did the janitor like to say about the floors that he had cleaned?**
   A. They were hard enough to hurt yourself on.
   B. They were shiny enough to see yourself in.
   C. They were slippery enough to skate on.
   D. They were clean enough to eat off of.

3. Why was Mrs. MacGrady not paying attention to Arthur?

A. She was texting on her mobile phone.

B. She was talking on the phone.

C. She was watching TV while cooking.

D. She was listening to music while cooking.

4. What happened when Arthur set down the bag of quarters?

A. He accidentally knocked over the bag of baking soda into it.

B. He accidentally knocked over the bag of chocolate chips into it.

C. He accidentally knocked over the bag of flour into it.

D. He accidentally knocked over the bag of sugar into it.

5. Why was Arthur is such a hurry to leave?

A. His mother was waiting and would be upset.

B. Buster was waiting and would be upset.

C. He needed to get home to meet a friend.

D. He wanted to go home and sleep.

$$\frac{372 \text{ words}}{\text{reading time ( ) sec}} \times 60 = (\qquad) \text{ WPM}$$

Build Your Vocabulary

detective [ditéktiv] n. 탐정, 형사
A detective is someone whose job is to discover what has happened in a crime or other situation and to find the people involved.

cafeteria [kæfətíəriə] n. 셀프 서비스식 식당, 구내식당
A cafeteria is a restaurant where you choose your food from a counter and take it to your table after paying for it.

janitor [dʒǽnitər] n. 수위, 관리인
A janitor is a person whose job is to look after a building.

eat off (of) idiom ~에 차린 것을 먹다; 먹어 치우다
If you eat off something, such as a plate, bowl or cup, you eat food on them.

prefer [prifə́ːr] v. (다른 것보다) ~을 더 좋아하다, 선호하다
If you prefer someone or something, you like that person or thing better than another, and so you are more likely to choose them if there is a choice.

plate [pleit] n. 접시, 그릇
A plate is a round or oval flat dish that is used to hold food.

be on the phone idiom (전화로) 통화 중이다
If you say that someone is on the phone, you mean that they are speaking to someone else by phone.

chief [tʃiːf] n. (단체의) 최고위자; n. (계급·직급상) 최고위자인
The chief of an organization is the person who is in charge of it.

wave [weiv] v. 흔들다, 신호하다; 파도치다; n. 파도, 물결
If you wave or wave your hand, you move your hand from side to side in the air, usually in order to say hello or goodbye to someone.

attention [əténʃən] n. 주의, 관심; 배려
If you give someone or something your attention, you look at it, listen to it, or think about it carefully.

patient [péiʃənt] a. 인내심[참을성] 있는; n. 환자
If you are patient, you stay calm and do not get annoyed, for example when something takes a long time, or when someone is not doing what you want them to do.

counter [káuntər] n. (부엌의) 조리대; 계산대, 판매대; (요리점·간이 식당 등의) 카운터
A counter is a piece of furniture that stands at the side of a dining room, having shelves and drawers.

bake [beik] v. (빵 등을) 굽다; 구워지다 (baking a. 빵 굽는 데 쓰는)
When a cake or bread bakes or when you bake it, it cooks in the oven without any extra liquid or fat.

ingredient [ingríːdiənt] n. 재료, 성분, 원료
Ingredients are the things that are used to make something, especially all the different foods you use when you are cooking a particular dish.

flour [flauər] n. 밀가루; 분말, 가루
Flour is a white or brown powder that is made by grinding grain, which is used to make bread, cakes, and pastry.

stick [stik] ① n. 막대 (모양의 것) ② v. 붙이다, 달라붙다; 찔러 넣다, 찌르다
A stick of something is a long thin piece of it.

square [skwɛər] n. 정사각형; a. 정사각형 모양의
A square is a shape with four sides that are all the same length and four corners that are all right angles.

firefighter [fáiərfàitər] n. 소방관
Firefighters are people whose job is to put out fires.

complex [kámpleks] n. 콤플렉스, 강박 관념; a. 복잡한
If someone has a complex about something, they have a mental or emotional problem relating to it, often because of an unpleasant experience in the past.

sensitive [sénsətiv] a. 민감한, 예민한; 감수성이 강한
If you are sensitive about something, you are easily worried and offended when people talk about it.

accidental [æksədéntl] a. 우연한; 부수적인 (accidentally ad. 우연히)
An accidental event happens by chance or as the result of an accident, and is not deliberately intended.

knock over idiom 쳐서 뒤엎다, 넘어뜨리다
If you knock something over, you push or hit it, making it fall or turn on its side.

quarter [kwɔ́:rtər] n. 25센트; 4분의 1; 15분
A quarter is an American or Canadian coin that is worth 25 cents.

harm [ha:rm] n. 해, 손해; vt. 해치다, 손상을 입히다
Harm is the damage to something which is caused by a particular course of action.

motion [móuʃən] n. 동작, 몸짓; v. 몸짓으로 알리다
A motion is an action, gesture, or movement.

turn away idiom 고개를 돌리다, 외면하다; ~를 돌려보내다
When you turn away, you move your body or part of your body so that it is facing in a different or opposite direction.

fit [fit] ① n. 욱하는 감정; 발작 (have a fit idiom 화나다) ② v. 꼭 맞다, 적합하다
If you say that someone will have a fit when they hear about something, you mean that they will be very angry or shocked.

be bound to idiom 반드시 ~하다, ~하게 마련이다

If you say that something is bound to happen or be true, you feel confident and certain of it.

Chapter 3

1. **Aside from looking for a mystery to solve, what was on Buster's mind at the arcade?**

   A. He wanted to find a way to earn quarters.

   B. He wanted a return match with a game.

   C. He wanted to finish him homework.

   D. He wanted to find a detective game.

2. **What item did Buster bring to the arcade?**

   A. Reading glasses

   B. A fingerprinting kit

   C. A magnifying glass

   D. A powder kit

3. **What did Buster find on Arthur's shirt?**

A. Flour

B. Powdered sugar

C. Ketchup

D. Dust

4. **What was the last kind of game that Arthur played at the arcade?**

A. Shooting

B. Hockey

C. Racing

D. Pinball

5. **Why was Buster so excited when he left the arcade?**

A. Arthur had hit the high score.

B. He had won a grand prize.

C. He had finally found a mystery.

D. He was having his favorite dessert.

$$\frac{524\ words}{reading\ time\ (\qquad)\ sec} \times 60 = (\qquad)\ WPM$$

Build Your Vocabulary

arcade [a:rkéid] n. 오락실, 게임 센터
An arcade is a commercial establishment featuring rows of coin-operated games.

return match [ritə́:rn mæʧ] n. 재시합, 설욕전
A return match is the second of two matches that are played by two sports teams or two players.

alien [éiljən] n. 외계인, 우주인; a. 진기한, 이질적인; 외국의, 이국의
In science fiction, an alien is a creature from outer space.

explore [iksplɔ́:r] v. 탐사하다, 탐험하다 (explorer n. 탐사자, 탐험가)
If you explore a place, you travel around it to find out what it is like.

rough up idiom ~을 두들겨 패다; 신경질나게 하다
If you rough someone up, you treat them violently by hittingor kicking, especially in order to frighten or warn them.

teach a lesson idiom ~에게 교훈을 가르치다, 따끔한 맛을 보이다
If you say that you are going to teach someone a lesson, you mean that you are going to punish them for something that they have done so that they do not do it again.

solve [salv] v. (수학 문제 등을) 풀다, 해결하다
If you solve a problem or a question, you find a solution or an answer to it.

draw [drɔ:] v. 끌다, 당기다; 그리다 n. 추첨, 제비뽑기
If someone or something draws you, it attracts you very strongly.

shifty [ʃífti] a. 간사해 보이는, 교활한
Someone who looks shifty gives the impression of being dishonest.

character [kǽriktər] n. 사람, 인물; 성격, 특성
You use character to say what kind of person someone is.

garbage [gá:rbidʒ] n. 쓰레기, 찌꺼기
Garbage is rubbish, especially waste from a kitchen.

dump [dʌmp] n. 쓰레기 더미; vt. 쏟아 버리다, 아무렇게나 내려놓다
A dump is a place where rubbish is left, for example on open ground outside a town.

figure [fígjər] v. 생각하다, 판단하다; 계산하다; n. 형태, 형상; 수치, 숫자
If you figure that something is the case, you think or guess that it is the case.

lookout [lúkaut] n. 경계, 감시
If someone keeps a lookout, especially on a boat, they look around all the time in order to make sure there is no danger.

magnifying glass [mǽgnəfàiŋ glæs] n. 확대경, 돋보기
A magnifying glass is a piece of glass which makes objects appear bigger than they actually are.

peer [piər] vi. 눈여겨보다, 응시하다
If you peer at something, you look at it very hard, usually because it is difficult to see clearly.

stuff [stʌf] n. 것(들), 물건, 물질; v. 채워 넣다, 채우다
You can use stuff to refer to things such as a substance, a collection of things, events, or ideas, or the contents of something in a general way without mentioning the thing itself by name.

definite [défənit] a. 확실한, 확고한; 분명한, 뚜렷한 (definitely ad. 확실히, 명확히)
If something such as a decision or an arrangement is definite, it is firm and clear, and unlikely to be changed.

quarter [kwɔ́:rtər] n. 25센트; 4분의 1; 15분
A quarter is an American or Canadian coin that is worth 25 cents.

cafeteria [kæfətíəriə] n. 셀프 서비스식 식당, 구내식당
A cafeteria is a restaurant where you choose your food from a counter and take it to your table after paying for it.

accidental [æ̀ksədéntl] a. 우연한; 부수적인 (accidentally ad. 우연히)
An accidental event happens by chance or as the result of an accident, and is not deliberately intended.

spill [spil] v. 엎지르다, 흘리다; n. 엎지름, 유출
If a liquid spills or if you spill it, it accidentally flows over the edge of a container.

flour [flauər] n. 밀가루; 분말, 가루
Flour is a white or brown powder that is made by grinding grain, which is used to make bread, cakes, and pastry.

disappoint [dìsəpɔ́int] v. 실망시키다, 낙담시키다 (disappointed a. 실망한, 좌절된)
If things or people disappoint you, they are not as good as you had hoped, or do not do what you hoped they would do.

make the rounds idiom 순회하다
If you make the rounds or do the rounds, you visit a series of different places.

survive [sərváiv] v. 살아남다, 생존하다
If a person or living thing survives in a dangerous situation such as an accident or an illness, they do not die.

get through idiom (곤란 등을) 벗어나다, 통과하다
If you get through, you survive a difficult or unpleasant experience or period in your life.

haunt [hɔːnt] v. (유령이) 출몰하다; (생각 따위가) 계속 떠오르다, 늘 따라다니다
(haunted a. 유령이 자주 나오는)
A ghost or spirit that haunts a place or a person regularly appears in the place, or is seen by the person and frightens them.

mangy [méindʒi] a. 지저분한, 초라한
A mangy animal looks dirty, uncared for or ill.

mutant [mjuːtnt] n. 돌연변이, 변종
A mutant is an animal or plant that is physically different from others of the same species because of a change in its genes.

revenge [rivéndʒ] n. 복수, 보복; vt. 복수하다, 원수를 갚다
Revenge involves hurting or punishing someone who has hurt or harmed you.

do (someone) in idiom (남을) 죽이다; (남을) 기진맥진하게 하다
If something does you in, it kills you or makes you feel extremely tired.

knob [nab] n. 손잡이
A knob is a round handle on a door or drawer which you use in order to open or close it.

release [rilíːs] vt. 놓아주다, 해방시키다, 풀어놓다; n. 석방
If you release someone or something, you stop holding them.

shoot [ʃuːt] v. (shot-shot) 힘차게 움직이다; 쏘다, 발사하다; n. 사격, 발포; int. 말해라
If someone or something shoots in a particular direction, they move in that direction quickly and suddenly.

slot [slat] n. (가늘고 긴) 구멍, 홈
A slot is a narrow opening in a machine or container, for example a hole that you put coins in to make a machine work.

ramp [ræmp] n. 경사로, 비탈길
A ramp is a sloping surface between two places that are at different levels.

ricochet [rikəʃéi] v. ~에 스치고 튀어 나오다; n. 스쳐 날기
When a bullet ricochets, it hits a surface and bounces away from it.

platform [plǽtfɔ:rm] n. 단, 대(臺); 승강장
A platform is a flat raised structure or area, usually one which something can stand on or land on.

downward [dáunwərd] ad. 아래쪽으로; a. 아래쪽으로 내려가는, 하향의
If you move or look downward, you move or look toward the ground or a lower level.

flip [flip] v. 홱 뒤집(히)다; 톡 던지다; (책장을) 휙휙 넘기다; n. 톡 던지기; 공중제비
If something flips over, or if you flip it over or into a different position, it moves or is moved into a different position.

keep it up idiom 계속 해나가다, 노력하다
Keep it up is used to tell someone to continue doing something as well as they are already doing it.

light [lait] v. (lit/lighted–lit/lighted) 빛을 비추다; 불을 붙이다, 불이 붙다; n. 빛
To light up means to become or to make something bright with light or color.

watch out idiom 조심해라!
You say 'watch out', when you warn someone about something dangerous.

on a roll idiom 승승장구 하고 있다
If you are on a roll, you are experiencing a period of success at what you are doing.

dodge [dadʒ] v. (재빨리) 피하다, 날쌔게 비키다, 몸을 홱 피하다; n. 발뺌
If you dodge, you move suddenly, often to avoid being hit, caught, or seen.

sink [siŋk] v. (sank/sunken–sunk/sunken) 가라앉다, 빠지다
If something sinks, it disappears below the surface of a mass of water.

initial [iníʃəl] n. (이름·명칭의) 머리글자, 첫 글자
Initials are the capital letters which begin each word of a name. For example, if your full name is Michael Dennis Stocks, your initials will be M.D.S.

pound [paund] v. 치다, 두드리다; (가슴이) 쿵쿵 뛰다; (머리가) 지끈거리다
If you pound something or pound on it, you hit it with great force, usually loudly and repeatedly.

onlooker [ɔ́:nlúkər] n. 구경꾼; 방관자
An onlooker is someone who watches an event take place but does not take part in it.

cheer [tʃiər] v. 환호성을 지르다, 응원하다; n. 환호(성)
When people cheer, they shout loudly to show their approval or to encourage someone who is doing something such as taking part in a game.

proud [praud] a. 자랑스러워하는, 자랑스러운 (**proudly** ad. 자랑스럽게)
If you feel proud, you feel pleased about something good that you possess or have done.

one and all idiom 모두, 누구나 다
One and all refers to everyone in a particular group.

Chapter 4

1. **How was Buster starting to feel about finding mysteries?**

   A. He was starting to feel a little down.

   B. He was starting to feel a little excited.

   C. He was starting to feel a little encouraged.

   D. He was starting to feel a little doubtful.

2. **Why did Mr. Haney, the principal, stop Arthur?**

   A. He reminded Arthur to give the quarters to him.

   B. He reminded Arthur to give the quarters to Mrs. MacGrady.

   C. He reminded Arthur to collect more quarters for the fire department.

   D. He reminded Arthur to stop playing games at the arcade.

3. **What punishment did Arthur face if the quarters were not found?**

   A. One day of after-school detention

   B. One week of after-school detention

   C. One day of after-school detention and no picnic

   D. One week of after-school detention and no picnic

4. **How did Buster offer to help Arthur?**

   A. He offered to hire a detective.

   B. He offered to find a detective.

   C. He offered to solve the case.

   D. He offered to bring him back food from the picnic.

5. **What did Arthur make Buster promise him?**

   A. He made Buster promise that he would solve it in one day.

   B. He made Buster promise that he would not get into deeper trouble.

   C. He made Buster promise that he would not spend too much money.

   D. He made Buster promise that he would find a better detective for him.

Check Your Reading Speed

1분에 몇 단어를 읽는지 리딩 속도를 측정해보세요.

$$\frac{557 \ words}{reading \ time \ (\quad) \ sec} \times 60 = (\quad) \ WPM$$

Build Your Vocabulary

admit [ædmít] v. 인정하다

If you admit that something bad, unpleasant, or embarrassing is true, you agree, often unwillingly, that it is true.

investigate [invéstəgèit] v. 수사하다, 조사하다

If someone, especially an official, investigates an event, situation, or claim, they try to find out what happened or what is the truth.

detective [ditéktiv] n. 탐정, 형사

A detective is someone whose job is to discover what has happened in a crime or other situation and to find the people involved.

aside [əsáid] ad. 한쪽으로; ~외에는

If you move something aside, you move it to one side of you.

wizard [wízərd] n. 귀재, 천재; 마법사

If you admire someone because they are very good at doing a particular thing, you can say that they are a wizard.

comment [káment] n. 논평, 언급; v. 논평하다, 견해를 밝히다

A comment is something that you say which expresses your opinion of something or which gives an explanation of it.

hall [hɔːl] n. (건물의) 복도, 통로; (건물 입구 안쪽의) 현관; 넓은 방[건물]

A hall in a building is a long passage with doors into rooms on both sides of it.

embarrass [imbǽrəs] v. 부끄럽게[무안하게] 하다; 어리둥절하게 하다, 당황하다
(embarrassing a. 쑥스러운)
If something or someone embarrasses you, they make you feel shy or ashamed.

modest [mɑ́dist] a. 겸손한; 얌전한, 수수한
If you say that someone is modest, you approve of them because they do not talk much about their abilities or achievements.

deserve [dizə́ːrv] vt. ~을 할[받을] 만하다, ~할 가치가 있다
If you say that a person or thing deserves something, you mean that they should have it or receive it because of their actions or qualities.

attention [ətén∫ən] n. 주의, 관심; 배려
If you give someone or something your attention, you look at it, listen to it, or think about it carefully.

sigh [sai] v. 한숨 쉬다; n. 한숨, 탄식
When you sigh, you let out a deep breath, as a way of expressing feelings such as disappointment, tiredness, or pleasure.

nimble [nimbl] a. (손·발 등이) 재빠른, 날렵한; 눈치 빠른, 영리한
Someone who is nimble is able to move their fingers, hands, or legs quickly and easily.

hawk [hɔːk] n. [조류] 매
A hawk is a large bird with a short, hooked beak, sharp claws, and very good eyesight.

reflex [ríːfleks] n. (pl.) 반사 신경; 반사 작용, 반사 운동
Your reflexes are your ability to react quickly with your body when something unexpected happens, for example when you are involved in sport or when you are driving a car.

principal [prínsəpəl] n. 장(長), 교장; a. 주요한, 제1의
The principal of a school is the person in charge of the school.

wave [weiv] v. 흔들다, 신호하다; 파도치다; n. 파도, 물결
If you wave or wave your hand, you move your hand from side to side in the air, usually in order to say hello or goodbye to someone.

quarter [kwɔ́:rtər] n. 25센트; 4분의 1; 15분
A quarter is an American or Canadian coin that is worth 25 cents.

collect [kəlékt] v. 모금하다; 모으다, 수집하다
If you collect for a charity or for a present for someone, you ask people to give you money for it.

fund [fʌnd] n. (특정 목적을 위한) 기금, 자금; v. 자금을 제공하다
Funds are amounts of money that are available to be spent, especially money that is given to an organization or person for a particular purpose.

drive [draiv] n. (조직적인) 모금 운동; 드라이브, 자동차 여행; v. (차를) 몰다, 운전하다
A drive is a special effort made by a group of people for a particular purpose.

secretary [sékrətèri] n. 비서; 서기, 사무관
A secretary is a person who is employed to do office work, such as typing letters, answering phone calls, and arranging meetings.

frown [fraun] v. 얼굴[눈살]을 찌푸리다; n. 찡그림, 찌푸림
When someone frowns, their eyebrows become drawn together, because they are annoyed or puzzled.

odd [ad] a. 이상한, 기묘한
If you describe someone or something as odd, you think that they are strange or unusual.

steal [sti:l] v. (stole-stolen) 훔치다, 도둑질하다
If you steal something from someone, you take it away from them without their permission and without intending to return it.

contain [kəntéin] a. 자제하다, 억누르다; 들어 있다, 포함하다
If you cannot contain a feeling such as excitement or anger, or if you cannot contain yourself, you cannot prevent yourself from showing your feelings.

^복_습 **arcade** [aːrkéid] n. 오락실, 게임 센터
An arcade is a commercial establishment featuring rows of coin-operated games.

go on idiom (잠깐 쉬었다가) 말을 계속하다; (어떤 상황이) 계속되다
If someone goes one, they continue speaking after a short pause.

[★]_★ **cost** [kɔːst] v. (사람에게 ~을) 잃게 하다, 비용이 들다; n. 비용, 값; 희생
If an event or mistake costs you something, you lose that thing as the result of it.

_★ **fortune** [fɔ́ːrtʃən] n. 큰 돈, 재산; 운수, 행운
You can refer to a large sum of money as a fortune or a small fortune to emphasize how large it is.

_★ **stare** [stɛər] v. 응시하다, 뚫어지게 보다
If you stare at someone or something, you look at them for a long time.

_★ **responsible** [rispánsəbl] a. 책임이 있는, 책임지고 있는
If you are responsible for something, it is your job or duty to deal with it and make decisions relating to it.

[★]_★ **certain** [sə́ːrtn] a. 확실한, 틀림없는 (certainly ad. 틀림없이, 분명히)
If you are certain about something, you firmly believe it is true and have no doubt about it.

_★ **shrink** [ʃriŋk] v. (shrank–shrunk) 움츠러들다, 오그라들다
If something shrinks or something else shrinks it, it becomes smaller.

_★ **farther** [fáːrðər] ad. 더 멀리, 더 나아가서; a. 더 먼
Farther means more distant in especially space or time.

_★ **stern** [stəːrn] a. 엄한, 단호한
Someone who is stern is very serious and strict.

^복_습 **cafeteria** [kæfətíəriə] n. 셀프 서비스식 식당, 구내식당
A cafeteria is a restaurant where you choose your food from a counter and take it to your table after paying for it.

counter [káuntər] n. (부엌의) 조리대; 계산, 판매대; (요리점·간이 식당 등의) 카운터
A counter is a piece of furniture that stands at the side of a dining room, having shelves and drawers.

turn up idiom 나타나다, 발견되다
If something that is hidden or lost turns up, it is found, especially by accident.

serve [səːrv] v. (어떤 기간을) 복역하다, 치르다; (상품·서비스·음식을) 제공하다
If you serve something such as a prison sentence, you spend a period of time doing it.

throat [θrout] n. 목구멍; 목 (clear one's throat idiom 목을 가다듬다, 헛기침하다)
Your throat is the back of your mouth and the top part of the tubes that go down into your stomach and your lungs.

detention [diténʃən] n. (학생에 대한 벌로서) 방과 후 남게 하기; 구금
Detention is a punishment for naughty schoolchildren, who are made to stay at school after the other children have gone home.

pause [pɔːz] vi. 중단하다, 잠시 멈추다; n. 멈춤, 중지
If you pause while you are doing something, you stop for a short period and then continue.

horrify [hɔ́ːrəfài] vt. 충격을 주다, 소름끼치게 하다 (horrified a. 겁에 질린, 충격 받은)
If someone is horrified, they feel shocked or disgusted, because of something that they have seen or heard.

rush [rʌʃ] v. 돌진하다, 급히 움직이다, 서두르다
If you rush something, you do it in a hurry, often too quickly and without much care.

thief [θiːf] n. 도둑, 절도범
A thief is a person who steals something from another person.

innocent [ínəsənt] a. 아무 잘못이 없는, 결백한; 순결한, 순진한
If someone is innocent, they did not commit a crime which they have been accused of.

solve [salv] v. (수학 문제 등을) 풀다, 해결하다
If you solve a problem or a question, you find a solution or an answer to it.

case [keis] n. 사건, 경우, 사례
A case is a crime or mystery that the police are investigating.

awake [əwéik] a. 잠들지 않은, 깨어 있는
Someone who is awake is not sleeping.

pajamas [pədʒá:məz] n. 파자마, 잠옷
A pair of pyjamas consists of loose trousers and a loose jacket that people, especially men, wear in bed.

trust [trʌst] v. (사람을) 신뢰하다, 믿다; n. 신뢰, 신임
If you trust someone, you believe that they are honest and sincere and will not deliberately do anything to harm you.

stuff [stʌf] n. 것(들), 물건, 물질; v. 채워 넣다, 채우다
You can use stuff to refer to things such as a substance, a collection of things, events, or ideas, or the contents of something in a general way without mentioning the thing itself by name.

as it is idiom 현 상황에서는, 지금 실정으로는
You use expression 'as it is' when you are making a contrast between a possible situation and what actually happened or is the case.

Chapter 5

1. **Who was the key witness in Buster's case?**

   A. Mr. Haney

   B. Mr. Morris

   C. Mrs. Baxter

   D. Mrs. MacGrady

2. **Who was Buster told to speak to next after the key witness?**

   A. Mrs. MacGrady

   B. Mr. Morris

   C. Mr. Haney

   D. Mrs. Baxter

3. Why had Mrs. MacGrady called Mr. Morris to the kitchen?

   A. She needed a lightbulb in the kitchen changed.

   B. She needed the machine mixing the brownie batter fixed.

   C. She needed the floor covered with brownie batter cleaned.

   D. She needed the oven where the brownies were baked to be turned on.

4. What was the source of the jingling sound from Mr. Morris?

   A. A lot of quarters

   B. His phone

   C. His keys

   D. His wallet

5. How did Buster feel about the case after talking to Mr. Morris?

   A. He felt that Arthur might have stolen the quarters.

   B. He felt that the case was becoming more complicated.

   C. He felt that the case was be solved very soon.

   D. He felt that he deserved a reward from Arthur if he solved the case.

1분에 몇 단어를 읽는지 리딩 속도를 측정해보세요.

$$\frac{589 \text{ words}}{\text{reading time ( ) sec}} \times 60 = (\quad) \text{ WPM}$$

Build Your Vocabulary

case [keis] n. 사건, 경우, 사례
A case is a crime or mystery that the police are investigating.

key [kiː] a. 가장 중요한, 핵심적인; n. 열쇠; (피아노) 건반
The key person or thing in a group is the most important one.

witness [wítnis] n. 목격자, 증인; v. 목격하다; 증언하다
A witness to an event such as an accident or crime is a person who saw it.

occupation [àkjupéiʃən] n. 직업, 업무; 점령, 점거
Your occupation is your job or profession.

cafeteria [kæfətíəriə] n. 셀프 서비스식 식당, 구내식당
A cafeteria is a restaurant where you choose your food from a counter and take it to your table after paying for it.

ingredient [ingríːdiənt] n. 재료, 성분, 원료
Ingredients are the things that are used to make something, especially all the different foods you use when you are cooking a particular dish.

bowl [boul] n. 사발, 그릇
A bowl is a round container with a wide uncovered top.

investigate [invéstəgèit] v. 수사하다, 조사하다
If someone, especially an official, investigates an event, situation, or claim, they try to find out what happened or what is the truth.

disappearance [dìsəpíːərəns] n. 실종, 사라짐; 소실, 소멸
If you refer to someone's disappearance, you are referring to the fact that nobody knows where they have gone.

quarter [kwɔ́ːrtər] n. 25센트; 4분의 1; 15분
A quarter is an American or Canadian coin that is worth 25 cents.

whereabouts [hwɛ́ərəbàuts] n. 소재, 행방
If you refer to the whereabouts of a particular person or thing, you mean the place where that person or thing maybe found.

fancy [fǽnsi] a. 고급스러운, 화려한; v. 원하다, ~하고 싶다; n. 공상, 상상
If you describe something as fancy, you mean that it is special, unusual, or elaborate, for example because it has a lot of decoration.

taste [teist] v. 맛보다, 시식하다; n. 맛, 풍미
If you can taste something that you are eating or drinking, you are aware of its flavor.

evidence [évədəns] n. 증거, 흔적; v. 증거가 되다, 증언하다
Evidence is anything that you see, experience, read, or are told that causes you to believe that something is true or has really happened.

wave [weiv] v. 흔들다, 신호하다; 파도치다; n. 파도, 물결
If you wave something, you hold it up and move it rapidly from side to side.

spatula [spǽtʃulə] n. 주걱
A spatula is an object like a knife with a wide, flat blade.

squirt [skwəːrt] v. (액체·분말 등을) 찍 짜다, 뿌리다; n. 분출
If you squirt a liquid somewhere or if it squirts somewhere, the liquid comes out of a narrow opening in a thin fast stream.

whip [hwip] v. (크림 등을) 휘저어 거품을 내다; 채찍질하다
(whipped cream n. 거품을 낸 크림)
When you whip something liquid such as cream or an egg, you stir it very fast until it is thick or stiff.

chief [tʃi:f] n. (단체의) 최고위자; n. (계급·직급상) 최고위자인
The chief of an organization is the person who is in charge of it.

jam [dʒæm] n. 작동하지 못하게 되다; 밀어 넣다; n. 고장; 혼잡
If something such as a part of a machine jams, or if something jams it, the part becomes fixed in position and is unable to move freely or work properly.

overflow [òuvərflóu] v. 넘치다, 넘쳐 흐르다; n. 넘쳐 흐름, 범람
If a liquid or a river overflows, it flows over the edges of the container or place that it is in.

mop [map] v. 대걸레로 닦다; n. 대걸레, 자루걸레
If you mop a surface such as a floor, you clean it with a mop.

mess [mes] n. 엉망진창, 난잡함; v. 망쳐놓다, 방해하다
If you say that something is a mess or in a mess, you think that it is in an untidy state.

pop [pap] v. 쏙 넣다; 불쑥 나타나다; 뻥 하고 터뜨리다; n. 뻥[탁] 하는 소리; 발포
If you pop something somewhere, you put it there quickly.

suggest [səgdʒést] vt. 제안하다; 암시하다
If you suggest something, you put forward a plan or idea for someone to think about.

mumble [mʌmbl] v. (불명확하게) 웅얼거리다, 중얼거리다; n. 중얼거림
If you mumble, you speak very quietly and not at all clearly with the result that the words are difficult to understand.

janitor [dʒǽnitər] n. 수위, 관리인
A janitor is a person whose job is to look after a building.

hallway [hɔ́:lwèi] n. 복도, 통로; 현관
A hallway in a building is a long passage with doors into rooms on both sides of it.

shoot [ʃu:t] int. 말해라; v. 쏘다, 발사하다; 힘차게 움직이다; n. 사격, 발포
People say 'shoot' to ask someone begin talking.

sequence [síːkwəns] n. (일련의) 연속적인 사건들; (사건·행동 등의) 순서
A sequence of events or things is a number of events or things that come one after another in a particular order.

previous [príːviəs] a. 앞의, 이전의
You refer to the period of time or the thing immediately before the one that you are talking about as the previous one.

detective [ditéktiv] n. 탐정, 형사
A detective is someone whose job is to discover what has happened in a crime or other situation and to find the people involved.

beam [biːm] v. 활짝 웃다; 비추다; n. 환한 미소; 빛줄기
If you say that someone is beaming, you mean that they have a big smile on their face because they are happy, pleased, or proud about something.

serious [síəriəs] a. 진지한; 심각한; 중요한, 중대한
Serious people are thoughtful and quiet, and do not laugh very often.

suspicious [səspíʃəs] a. 의심하는, 수상쩍은 (suspiciously ad. 수상쩍은 듯이)
If you are suspicious of someone or something, you believe that they are probably involved in a crime or some dishonest activity.

lightbulb [láitbʌlb] n. 백열전구
A lightbulb is the round glass part of an electric light or lamp which light shines from.

batter [bǽtər] n. [요리] 반죽; v. 반죽하다
Batter is a mixture of flour, eggs, and milk that is used in cooking.

fold [fould] v. (손·팔·다리를) 끼다, 포개다; 접다, 접어 포개다
If you fold your arms or hands, you bring them together and cross or link them, for example over your chest.

tidy [táidi] a. (성질 등이) 깔끔한; 잘 정돈된; v. 정리하다
Someone who is tidy likes everything to be neat and arranged in an organized way.

as a rule idiom 일반적으로, 대개
If you say that something happens as a rule, you mean that it usually happens.

favor [féivər] n. 호의; 친절한 행위; vt. 더 좋아하다, 선호하다; 편들다
If you do someone a favor, you do something for them even though you do not have to.

whatever you say idiom 당신 뜻대로[좋을 대로] (하겠다)
Whatever you say is used to agree to someone's suggestion because you do not want to argue.

bucket [bʌ́kit] n. 양동이
A bucket is a round metal or plastic container with a handle attached to its sides.

jingle [dʒíŋgl] v. 짤랑짤랑 소리를 내다; n. 딸랑딸랑 울리는 소리
When something jingles or when you jingle it, it makes a gentle ringing noise, like small bells.

catch up idiom 따라잡다, 따라가다
If you catch up with someone, you reach them by walking faster than them.

huge [hjuːdʒ] a. (크기·양·정도가) 엄청난, 거대한
Something or someone that is huge is extremely large in size.

get to the bottom of idiom 진상을 규명하다, 해결하다
If you get to the bottom of something, you find the true cause of it or the solution to it.

dig [dig] v. (dug-dug) 파다, 파헤치다; n. 파기
If people or animals dig, they make a hole in the ground or in a pile of earth, stones, or rubbish.

complicated [kámplikèitid] a. 복잡한, 이해하기 어려운
If you say that something is complicated, you mean it has so many parts or aspects that it is difficult to understand or deal with.

✦✦✦ sight [sait] n. 눈으로 볼 수 있는 범위, 시야; 시력
If something is in sight, you can see it.

Chapter 6

1. **Who did Buster meet at the suspect's home?**

   A. The suspect's brother

   B. The suspect's sister

   C. The suspect's mother

   D. The suspect's dog

2. **What did D.W. have Buster write down?**

   A. She made him write down that the hat looked silly on him.

   B. She made him write down that he sounded silly as a detective.

   C. She made him write down that he was not a real detective.

   D. She made him write down that he would prove Arthur's innocence.

3. **How did D.W. feel about the idea of Arthur having brought the quarters home?**
   A. She thought that he already had enough money.
   B. She thought that the quarters were too heavy for Arthur to carry alone.
   C. She thought that Arthur would not have brought them inside the home.
   D. She thought that Arthur would have spent them all already.

4. **What did D.W. suggest Buster check?**
   A. The living room for signs of damage
   B. The garage for signs of hiding
   C. Arthur's room for signs of quarters
   D. The lawn for signs of digging

5. **What did Buster tell Arthur when D.W. walked by with a shovel?**
   A. He told Arthur that D.W. was searching for buried treasure.
   B. He told Arthur that D.W. was digging a garden.
   C. He told Arthur that he was better off not asking.
   D. He told Arthur that the case would soon be solved.

$$\frac{517 \ words}{reading \ time \ (\qquad) \ sec} \times 60 = (\qquad) \ WPM$$

Build Your Vocabulary

^{복습}aside [əsáid] ad. ~외에는; 한쪽으로
You use aside to indicate that you have finished talking about something, or that you are leaving it out of your discussion, and that you are about to talk about something else.

＊suspect [səspékt] n. 용의자, 혐의자; v. 의심하다
A suspect is a person who the police or authorities think may be guilty of a crime.

＊liar [laiər] n. 거짓말쟁이
If you say that someone is a liar, you mean that they tell lies.

＊support [səpɔ́:rt] vt. 지지하다, 유지하다; n. 지지, 받침
If you support someone or their ideas or aims, you agree with them, and perhaps help them because you want them to succeed.

＊scene [si:n] n. 장소, 현장; 장면
The scene of an event is the place where it happened.

cool customer [ku:l kʌ́stəmər] n. 뻔뻔한 녀석
A cool customer is someone who stays calm and does not show their emotions, even in a difficult situation.

＊handle [hǽndl] vt. 다루다, 처리하다; n. 손잡이, 핸들
If you say that someone can handle a problem or situation, you mean that they have the ability to deal with it successfully.

^{복습} **figure** [fígjər] v. 생각하다, 판단하다; 계산하다; n. 형태, 형상; 수치, 숫자
If you figure that something is the case, you think or guess that it is the case.

^{복습} **probably** [prábəbli] ad. 아마
If you say that something is probably the case, you think that it is likely to be the case, although you are not sure.

clear [kliər] v. (~의) 혐의를 벗기다; 깨끗이 하다; a. 분명한; 깨끗한
If someone is cleared, they are proved to be not guilty of a crime or mistake.

jail [dʒeil] n. 교도소, 감옥
A jail is a place where criminals are kept in order to punish them, or where people waiting to be tried are kept.

make a face idiom 얼굴을 찌푸리다, 침울한 표정을 짓다
If you make a face, you twist your face to indicate a certain mental or emotional state.

^{복습} **go on** idiom (잠깐 쉬었다가) 말을 계속하다; (어떤 상황이) 계속되다
If someone goes one, they continue speaking after a short pause.

pad [pæd] n. 필기첩, 메모지의 묶음
A pad of paper is a number of pieces of paper which are fixed together along the top or the side, so that each piece can be torn off when it has been used.

take down idiom ~을 적다, 기록하다; 해체하다
If you take down a note or a letter, you write down something you want to remember or the words that someone says.

^{복습} **nod** [nad] v. (고개를) 끄덕이다, 끄덕여 나타내다; n. (고개를) 끄덕임
If you nod, you move your head downward and upward to show agreement, understanding, or approval.

silly [síli] a. 어리석은, 바보 같은; n. 바보
If you say that someone or something is silly, you mean that they are foolish, childish, or ridiculous.

serious [síəriəs] a. 심각한; 중요한, 중대한; 진지한
Serious problems or situations are very bad and cause people to be worried or afraid.

besides [bisáidz] ad. 게다가, 뿐만 아니라; prep. ~외에
Besides something or beside something means in addition to it.

giggle [gigl] v. 낄낄 웃다; n. 낄낄 웃음
If someone giggles, they laugh in a childlike way, because they are amused, nervous, or embarrassed.

subject [sʌ́bdʒikt] n. (논의 등의) 주제, (다뤄지고 있는) 문제; 학과, 과목
The subject of something such as a conversation, letter, or book is the thing that is being discussed or written about.

third degree [θə:rd digrí:] n. (경찰의) 엄한 심문, 고문
If someone is given the third degree, they are questioned or criticized extremely severely, sometimes with physical violence.

certain [sə:rtn] a. 확실한, 틀림없는 (certainly ad. 틀림없이, 분명히)
If you are certain about something, you firmly believe it is true and have no doubt about it.

smoke screen [smóuk skrí:n] n. 연막, 위장
If something that you do or say is a smoke screen, it is intended to hide the truth about your activities or intentions.

stuff [stʌf] n. 것(들), 물건, 물질; v. 채워 넣다, 채우다
You can use stuff to refer to things such as a substance, a collection of things, events, or ideas, or the contents of something in a general way without mentioning the thing itself by name.

jingle [dʒiŋgl] v. 짤랑짤랑 소리를 내다; n. 딸랑딸랑 울리는 소리
When something jingles or when you jingle it, it makes a gentle ringing noise, like small bells.

absentminded [ǽbsəntmáindid] a. 얼빠진, 멍하니 있는
(absentmindedly ad. 방심하여, 멍하니, 넋을 잃고)
Someone who is absentminded forgets things or does not pay attention to what they are doing.

glare [glɛər] v. 노려보다, 쏘아보다; n. 노려봄
If you glare at someone, you look at them with an angry expression on your face.

on purpose idiom 고의로, 일부러
If you do something on purpose, you do it intentionally.

forgetful [fərgétfəl] a. 건망증이 있는, 잘 잊어버리는
Someone who is forgetful often forgets things.

possibility [pàsəbíləti] n. 가능성
If you say there is a possibility that something is the case or that something will happen, you mean that it might be the case or it might happen.

not that idiom 그렇게[그 정도로] ~하지는 않은
If something is not that bad, funny, or expensive for example, it is not as bad, funny, or expensive as it might be or as has been suggested.

close by idiom (~의) 가까이에
Something that is close by is near to you.

figure out idiom ~을 생각해내다, 발견하다
If you figure out a solution to a problem or the reason for something, you succeed in solving it or understanding it.

clever [klévər] a. 영리한, 똑똑한, 재기 넘치는
Someone who is clever is intelligent and able to understand things easily or plan things well.

scratch [skrætʃ] v. 긁다, 할퀴다; n. 생채기, 할큄, 찰과상
If you scratch yourself, you rub your fingernails against your skin because it is itching.

lawn [lɔːn] n. 잔디밭, 잔디
A lawn is an area of grass that is kept cut short and is usually part of someone's garden or backyard, or part of a park.

sign [sain] n. 흔적, 징후; 표지판, 간판; v. (서류·편지 등에) 서명하다
If there is a sign of something, there is something which shows that it exists or is happening.

recent [riːsnt] a. 근래의, 최근의; 새로운
A recent event or period of time happened only a short while ago.

dig [dig] v. 파다, 파헤치다; n. 파기
If people or animals dig, they make a hole in the ground or in a pile of earth, stones, or rubbish.

case [keis] n. 사건, 경우, 사례
A case is a crime or mystery that the police are investigating.

sigh [sai] v. 한숨 쉬다; n. 한숨, 탄식
When you sigh, you let out a deep breath, as a way of expressing feelings such as disappointment, tiredness, or pleasure.

thorough [θɔ́ːrou] a. 철저한, 주도면밀한; 완전한
A thorough action or activity is one that is done very carefully and in a detailed way so that nothing is forgotten.

detective [ditéktiv] n. 탐정, 형사
A detective is someone whose job is to discover what has happened in a crime or other situation and to find the people involved.

miss [mis] v. (어디에 참석하지 않아서 그 일을) 놓치다; (치거나 잡거나 닿지 못하고) 놓치다
If you miss something such as a meeting or an activity, you do not go to it or take part in it.

hesitate [hézətèit] v. 주저하다, 머뭇거리다, 망설이다
If you hesitate, you do not speak or act for a short time, usually because you are uncertain, embarrassed, or worried about what you are going to say or do.

shovel [ʃʌvəl] n. 삽; v. ~을 삽으로 뜨다, 삽으로 일하다
A shovel is a tool with a long handle that is used for lifting and moving earth, coal, or snow.

stare [stɛər] v. 응시하다, 뚫어지게 보다
If you stare at someone or something, you look at them for a long time.

be better off idiom ~하는 편이 낫다
If you say that someone would be better off doing something, you are advising them to do it or expressing the opinion that it would benefit them to do it.

Chapter 7

1. **How did Buster picture Arthur at the beginning of the chapter?**

   A. He pictured Arthur as an innocent victim.

   B. He pictured Arthur as an clueless victim.

   C. He pictured Arthur as a criminal mastermind.

   D. He pictured Arthur as a common criminal.

2. **Why was Buster not acting like normal at dinner?**

   A. He had a fever.

   B. He had a headache.

   C. He had not figured out how to help Arthur.

   D. He had not figured out how to finish his homework.

3. **What did Mrs. Baxter say about Buster and his work for Arthur?**

A. She said that she was sure Arthur appreciated it.

B. She said that Buster should let Arthur solve his own problem.

C. She said that she would help Buster solve the case.

D. She said that Arthur might not stay friends with Buster.

4. **What was Buster's big breakthrough when he called Arthur?**

A. The quarters were stolen by an army of evil teachers.

B. The quarters were stolen by an army of evil aliens.

C. The quarters were stolen by an army of evil monsters.

D. The quarters were stolen by an army of evil robots.

5. **What did Arthur suggest Buster do?**

A. He suggested that Buster take some medicine.

B. He suggested that Buster get some sleep.

C. He suggested that Buster get some food.

D. He suggested that Buster get some better ideas.

Check Your Reading Speed

1분에 몇 단어를 읽는지 리딩 속도를 측정해보세요.

$$\frac{508 \text{ words}}{\text{reading time (} \quad \text{) sec}} \times 60 = (\quad) \text{ WPM}$$

Build Your Vocabulary

☼ **criminal** [krímənl] a. 범죄의; n. 범죄자, 범인
A criminal is a person who regularly commits crimes.

mastermind [mǽstərmàind] n. 지휘[조종]하는 사람; v. 지휘하다, 조종하다
The mastermind behind a difficult or complicated plan, often a criminal one, is the person who is responsible for planning and organizing it.

☼ **picture** [píktʃər] v. 마음에 그리다, 상상하다; (그림으로) 그리다; n. 그림, 사진
If you picture something in your mind, you think of it and have such a clear memory or idea of it that you seem to be able to see it.

hideout [háidàut] n. 은신처, 아지트
A hideout is a place where someone goes secretly because they do not want anyone to find them, for example if they are running away from the police.

복습 **shiny** [ʃáini] a. 빛나는, 반짝거리는
Shiny things are bright and reflect light.

복습 **quarter** [kwɔ́:rtər] n. 25센트; 4분의 1; 15분
A quarter is an American or Canadian coin that is worth 25 cents.

☼ **drip** [drip] v. 방울방울[똑똑] 떨어지다; n. 방울져 떨어지는 것, (물)방울
When something drips, drops of liquid fall from it.

* insane [inséin] a. 제정신이 아닌, 미친 (insanely ad. 미친 듯이)
Someone who is insane has a mind that does not work in a normal way, with the result that their behavior is very strange.

be used to ~ing idiom ~하는 데에 익숙하다
If you are used to something or are used to doing something, you are familiar with it or are accustomed to it.

복습 nod [nad] v. (고개를) 끄덕이다, 끄덕여 나타내다; n. (고개를) 끄덕임
If you nod, you move your head downward and upward to show agreement, understanding, or approval.

* helping [hélpiŋ] n. (음식의) 한 그릇; 조력, 원조
A helping of food is the amount of it that you get in a single serving.

‡ dessert [dizə́:rt] n. 디저트, 후식
Dessert is something sweet, such as fruit or a pudding, that you eat at the end of a meal.

* headache [hédeik] n. 두통
If you have a headache, you have a pain in your head.

‡ fever [fí:vər] n. 열, 고열
If you have a fever when you are ill, your body temperature is higher than usual.

복습 case [keis] n. 사건, 경우, 사례
A case is a crime or mystery that the police are investigating.

복습 figure out idiom ~을 생각해내다, 발견하다
If you figure out a solution to a problem or the reason for something, you succeed in solving it or understanding it.

‡ appreciate [əprí:ʃièit] vt. 고맙게 생각하다; 평가하다, 감상하다
If you appreciate something that someone has done for you or is going to do for you, you are grateful for it.

detective [ditéktiv] n. 탐정, 형사
A detective is someone whose job is to discover what has happened in a crime or other situation and to find the people involved.

flip [flip] v. (책장을) 휙휙 넘기다; 톡 던지다; 홱 뒤집(히)다; n. 톡 던지기; 공중제비
If you flip through the pages of a book, for example, you quickly turn over the pages in order to find a particular one or to get an idea of the contents.

pad [pæd] n. 필기첩, 메모지의 묶음
A pad of paper is a number of pieces of paper which are fixed together along the top or the side, so that each piece can be torn off when it has been used.

clue [kluː] n. 단서, 실마리
A clue is a sign or some information which helps you to find the answer to a problem.

solve [salv] v. (수학 문제 등을) 풀다, 해결하다
If you solve a problem or a question, you find a solution or an answer to it.

picky [píki] a. 까다로운, 별스러운
Someone who is picky is difficult to please and only likes a small range of things.

ragged [rǽgid] a. 해진, 갈기갈기 찢긴; 초라한, 남루한
(ragged-round-the-edges a. 가장자리가 울퉁불퉁한)
You can say that something is ragged when it is untidy or uneven.

accept [æksépt] v. (기꺼이) 받아들이다
If you accept something that you have been offered, you say yes to it or agree to take it.

wonder [wʌ́ndər] v. 호기심을 가지다, 이상하게 여기다; n. 경탄할 만한 것, 경이
If you wonder about something, you think about it because it interests you and you want to know more about it, or because you are worried or suspicious about it.

‡ **report** [ripɔ́ːrt] v. 알리다, 발표하다, 전하다; n. 보도
If you report something that has happened, you tell people about it.

‡ **progress** [prágres] n. 진보, 향상; 전진, 진행; vi. 진보하다; 진행하다
Progress is the process of gradually improving or getting nearer to achieving or completing something.

‡ **inform** [infɔ́ːrm] v. 정보[지식]를 제공하다; 알려주다, 통지하다
(keep someone informed idiom 남에게 상세한 정보를 계속 주다)
If you inform someone of something, you tell them about it.

* **barely** [béərli] ad. 간신히, 가까스로, 빠듯하게
If you say that one thing had barely happened when something else happened, you mean that the first event was followed immediately by the second.

‡ **agree** [əgríː] v. 동의하다, 찬성하다
If you agree with an action or suggestion, you approve of it.

for sale idiom 팔려고 내놓은
If something is for sale, it is being offered to people to buy.

‡ **lie** [lai] v. (lay-lain) 누워 있다, 눕다; 거짓말하다; n. 거짓말
If you are lying somewhere, you are in a horizontal position and are not standing or sitting.

swirl [swəːrl] n. 소용돌이; v. 소용돌이 치다, 빙빙 돌다
A swirl is a whirling movement of something such as liquid or flowing.

‡ **involve** [inválv] v. (상황·사건·활동이 사람을) 관련시키다; 포함하다
If a situation or activity involves someone, they are taking part in it.

‡ **somehow** [sʌ́mhàu] ad. 여하튼, 어쨌든; 왠지, 아무래도
You use somehow to say that you do not know or cannot say how something was done or will be done.

‡ **crack** [kræk] v. (사건을) 풀다, 해결하다; 금이 가다, 깨다; n. 날카로운 소리; 갈라진 금
If you crack a problem or a code, you solve it, especially after a lot of thought.

leap [liːp] v. (leapt/leaped–leapt/leaped) 껑충 뛰다; 뛰어넘다; n. 뜀, 도약
(leap to one's feet idiom (기뻐서) 뛰어오르다, 벌떡 일어서다)
If you leap, you jump high in the air or jump a long distance.

dial [daiəl] v. 전화를 걸다, 다이얼을 돌리다; n. (시계·계기 등의) 문자반, 눈금판
If you dial, you turn the dial or press the buttons on a telephone in order to phone someone.

steal [stiːl] v. (stole–stolen) 훔치다, 도둑질하다
If you steal something from someone, you take it away from them without their permission and without intending to return it.

army [áːrmi] n. 부대, 집단; 군대, 육군
An army of people, animals, or things is a large number of them, especially when they are regarded as a force of some kind.

evil [íːvəl] a. 나쁜, 사악한; n. 악
If you describe something as evil, you mean that you think it causes a great deal of harm to people and is morally bad.

fuel [fjuːəl] n. 연료; v. 연료를 공급하다
Fuel is a substance such as coal, oil, or petrol that is burned to provide heat or power.

notice [nóutis] v. ~을 의식하다, 주목하다, 관심을 기울이다; n. 신경 씀, 주목
If you notice something or someone, you become aware of them.

transform [trænsfɔ́ːrm] v. ~을 (~으로) 바꾸다, 변형하다; n. 변형
To transform something into something else means to change or convert it into that thing.

shape [ʃeip] n. 모양, 형태; v. (어떤) 모양[형태]으로 만들다
The shape of an object, a person, or an area is the appearance of their outside edges or surfaces, for example whether they are round, square, curved, or fat.

sigh [sai] v. 한숨 쉬다; n. 한숨, 탄식
When you sigh, you let out a deep breath, as a way of expressing feelings such as disappointment, tiredness, or pleasure.

breakthrough [bréikθrù:] n. 획기적인 발전, 돌파구
A breakthrough is an important development or achievement.

depend [dipénd] v. ~에 달려있다, 좌우되다; 의존하다, 의지하다
If you say that one thing depends on another, you mean that the first
thing will be affected or determined by the second.

be in for idiom (특히 불쾌한 일을 곧) 맞게 될 상황이다
If you are in for something, you are going to experience something
unpleasant, for example a shock, a surprise, or trouble.

Chapter

8

1. **According to Buster, what kind of pain do detectives feel even when they are supposed to be tough?**

   A. The pain when a friend is fighting

   B. The pain when a friend is missing

   C. The pain when a friend is lonely

   D. The pain when a friend is hurting

2. **Why did Arthur ask if Buster was okay being seen with him?**

   A. People might have thought that Buster was Arthur's partner in crime.

   B. People might have thought that Buster did not know about the crime.

   C. Buster was supposed to be looking for clues on his own.

   D. Buster had given up on trying to help Arthur with his problem.

3. **What did Arthur say of Buster as a detective?**

   A. He said he might be a lazy detective.

   B. He said he might be a lousy detective.

   C. He said he might be a bad detective.

   D. He said he might be an expert detective.

4. **What did Mr. Ratburn say to Arthur before they left for the picnic?**

   A. He told Arthur that he would save some food from the picnic for him.

   B. He told Arthur to give up and just accept his punishment.

   C. He told Arthur that the truth would come out in the end.

   D. He told Arthur that he could return the quarters later to him.

5. **How did the Brain give Buster a clue to the case?**

   A. He said he enjoyed hot baths with water overflowing.

   B. He said that his morning cereal was often overflowing with milk.

   C. He said a sad movie made his heart feel like it was overflowing.

   D. He said a tough math problem made his brain feel like it was overflowing.

Check Your Reading Speed

1분에 몇 단어를 읽는지 리딩 속도를 측정해보세요.

$$\frac{498 \ words}{reading \ time \ (\quad) \ sec} \times 60 = (\quad) \ WPM$$

Build Your Vocabulary

detective [ditéktiv] n. 탐정, 형사
A detective is someone whose job is to discover what has happened in a crime or other situation and to find the people involved.

be supposed to ~ idiom (관습·법·의무로) ~하기로 되어 있다
If you are supposed to do something, you are expected or required to do something according to a rule, a custom or an arrangement.

tough [tʌf] a. 강인한, 억센; 곤란한, 어려운
A tough person is strong and determined, and can tolerate difficulty or suffering.

slump [slʌmp] n. (어깨가) 구부러짐; 쿵 떨어짐; v. 털썩 앉다; (수량·가격 등이) 급감하다
A slump is a bowed or bent position or posture, especially of the shoulders.

mess [mes] n. 엉망진창, 난잡함; v. 망쳐놓다, 방해하다
If you say that something is a mess or in a mess, you think that it is in an untidy state.

crime [kraim] n. 범행, 범죄
A crime is an illegal action or activity for which a person can be punished by law.

accomplice [əkámplis] n. 공범자, 연루자
Someone's accomplice is a person who helps them to commit a crime.

henchman [hénʧmən] n. 심복, 부하
If you refer to someone as another person's henchman, you mean that they work for or support the other person, especially by doing unpleasant, violent, or dishonest things on their behalf.

desert [dizə́ːrt] v. 버리다, 저버리다
If someone deserts you, they go away and leave you, and no longer help or support you.

rat [ræt] n. 배신자, 비열한 놈; 쥐
If you call someone a rat, you mean that you are angry with them or dislike them, often because they have cheated you or betrayed you.

sink [siŋk] v. 가라앉다, 빠지다 (sinking a. 가라앉는)
If something sinks, it disappears below the surface of a mass of water.

jail [dʒeil] n. 교도소, 감옥
A jail is a place where criminals are kept in order to punish them, or where people waiting to be tried are kept.

realize [ríːəlàiz] v. 깨닫다, 알아차리다
If you realize that something is true, you become aware of that fact or understand it.

miss [mis] v. (어디에 참석하지 않아서 그 일을) 놓치다; (치거나 잡거나 닿지 못하고) 놓치다
If you miss something such as a meeting or an activity, you do not go to it or take part in it.

innocent [ínəsənt] a. 아무 잘못이 없는, 결백한; 순결한, 순진한
If someone is innocent, they did not commit a crime which they have been accused of.

let down idiom 실망시키다, 낙심시키다; 낮추다, 내리다
If you let down someone, you disappoint them by failing to do what you agreed to do or were expected to do.

lousy [láuzi] a. 서투른, 형편없는; (몸·기분이) 안 좋은
If you describe someone as lousy, you mean that they are very bad at something they do.

motion [móuʃən] v. 몸짓으로 알리다; n. 동작, 몸짓

If you motion to someone, you move your hand or head as a way of telling them to do something or telling them where to go.

nod [nad] v. (고개를) 끄덕이다, 끄덕여 나타내다; n. (고개를) 끄덕임

If you nod, you move your head downward and upward to show agreement, understanding, or approval.

give up idiom 포기하다, 단념하다

If you give up, you decide that you cannot do something and stop trying to do it.

certain [sə́ːrtn] a. 확실한, 틀림없는 (certainly ad. 틀림없이, 분명히)

If you are certain about something, you firmly believe it is true and have no doubt about it.

bullhorn [búllhɔːrn] n. 휴대용 확성기, 핸드 마이크; v. 확성기로 말하다

A bullhorn is a device for making your voice sound louder in the open air.

board [bɔːrd] v. 승차하다, 탑승하다

When you board a train, ship, or aircraft, you get on it in order to travel somewhere.

forward [fɔ́ːrwərd] ad. (위치가) 앞으로; (시간상으로) 미래로

If you move or look forward, you move or look in a direction that is in front of you.

lawyer [lɔ́ːjər] n. 변호사

A lawyer is a person who is qualified to advise people about the law and represent them in court.

get (someone) off idiom (남에게) 처벌을 면하게 해주다

If you get someone off, you help them to escape punishment.

prove [pruːv] v. 입증하다, 증명하다; 드러나다, 판명되다

If you prove that something is true, you show by means of argument or evidence that it is definitely true.

clue [kluː] n. 단서, 실마리
A clue is a sign or some information which helps you to find the answer to a problem.

case [keis] n. 사건, 경우, 사례
A case is a crime or mystery that the police are investigating.

missing [mísiŋ] a. (제자리나 집에 있지 않고) 없어진; 빠진, 누락된
If something is missing, it is not in its usual place, and you cannot find it.

be all set idiom 준비가 되어 있다
If you are all set to do something, you are ready to do it or are likely to do it.

frown [fraun] v. 얼굴[눈살]을 찌푸리다; n. 찡그림, 찌푸림
When someone frowns, their eyebrows become drawn together, because they are annoyed or puzzled.

overflow [òuvərflóu] v. 넘치다, 넘쳐 흐르다; n. 넘쳐 흐름, 범람
If a liquid or a river overflows, it flows over the edges of the container or place it is in.

stare [stɛər] v. 응시하다, 뚫어지게 보다
If you stare at someone or something, you look at them for a long time.

pressure [préʃər] n. 압박감, 스트레스
If there is pressure on a person, someone is trying to persuade or force them to do something.

get to someone idiom ~를 괴롭히다
If something that has continued for some time gets to you, it starts causing you to suffer.

whisper [hwíspər] v. 속삭이다; n. 속삭임
When you whisper, you say something very quietly.

race [reis] ① v. 질주하다, 달리다; 경주하다; n. 경주 ② n. 인종, 민족
If you race somewhere, you go there as quickly as possible.

hold on idiom 기다려, 멈춰

People say 'hold on' to ask someone to wait or stop for a short time.

solve [salv] v. (수학 문제 등을) 풀다, 해결하다

If you solve a problem or a question, you find a solution or an answer to it.

Chapter

9

1. **According to Buster, how does every detective want to act at all times?**

    A. Cold, crazy, and careful

    B. Cool, calm, and collected

    C. Cool, careful, and comfortable

    D. Cool, cheerful, and calculated

2. **Which of the following was NOT one of the questions that Buster asked Mrs. MacGrady?**

    A. Did she use any new equipment?

    B. Had it ever overflowed before?

    C. Did she use a different recipe?

    D. Did she know how to make brownies?

3. Why did Buster take time explaining his point?

A. He was still thinking of a solution.

B. He wanted to describe it like a story.

C. He did not want to rush his moment of glory.

D. He wanted to make sure it was easy to understand.

4. How did Buster reveal where the quarters were?

A. He picked up a brownie and broke it in two.

B. He used a metal detector on the brownies.

C. He bit into a brownie and spit out a quarter.

D. He asked Mrs. MacGrady to try a brownie.

5. Why had the quarters ended up in the brownies?

A. Mrs. MacGrady had wanted to hide the quarters in a clever place.

B. Mrs. MacGrady had mistaken the bag of quarters for flour.

C. Arthur wanted to make a mystery for Buster to solve.

D. Arthur had thought it would be interesting to put money in food.

$$\frac{460 \ words}{reading \ time \ (\qquad) \ sec} \times 60 = (\qquad) \ WPM$$

Build Your Vocabulary

detective [ditéktiv] n. 탐정, 형사

A detective is someone whose job is to discover what has happened in a crime or other situation and to find the people involved.

collected [kəléktid] a. 아주 침착한, 태연한

If you say that someone is collected, you mean that they are very calm and self-controlled, especially when they are in a difficult or serious situation.

at all times idiom 항상, 언제나

If something happens at all times, it always happens.

sit back idiom (의자에) 편안히 앉다

If you're sitting back, you sit or lean comfortably in a chair.

fate [feit] n. 운명, 숙명

A person's or thing's fate is what happens to them.

pack [pæk] v. (짐을) 꾸리다, 포장하다

When you pack a bag, you put clothes and other things into it, because you are leaving a place or going on holiday.

carton [ka:rtn] n. (음식이나 음료를 담는) 곽, 통; 상자

A carton is a plastic or cardboard container in which food or drink is sold.

neat [niːt] a. 정돈된, 단정한, 말쑥한 (neatly ad. 깔끔하게, 말쑥하게)
A neat place, thing, or person is tidy and smart, and has everything in the correct place.

organize [ɔ́ːrgənàiz] v. 정리하다, 체계화하다; (어떤 일을) 계획하다, 준비하다
If you organize a set of things, you arrange them in an ordered way or give them a structure.

counter [káuntər] n. (부엌의) 조리대; 계산대, 판매대; (요리점·간이 식당 등의) 카운터
A counter is a piece of furniture that stands at the side of a dining room, having shelves and drawers.

sheet [ʃiːt] n. 한 판, 한 장; (침대 등의) 시트
A sheet of something is a thin wide layer of it over the surface of something else.

square [skwɛər] n. 정사각형; a. 정사각형 모양의
A square is a shape with four sides that are all the same length and four corners that are all right angles.

rush [rʌʃ] v. 돌진하다, 급히 움직이다, 서두르다
If you rush somewhere, you go there quickly.

arrest [ərést] v. 체포하다; 막다, 저지하다; n. 체포; 저지
If the police arrest you, they take charge of you and take you to a police station, because they believe you may have committed a crime.

speeding [spíːdiŋ] n. (차량의) 속도 위반
Speeding is the act or practice of exceeding the speed limit.

surprise [sərpráiz] v. 놀라게 하다, 경악하게 하다 (surprised a. 매우 놀란)
If you surprise someone, you give them, tell them, or do something they are not expecting.

throat [θrout] n. 목구멍; 목 (clear one's throat idiom 목을 가다듬다, 헛기침하다)
Your throat is the back of your mouth and the top part of the tubes that go down into your stomach and your lungs.

follow up on idiom ~을 계속하다, 끝까지 하다
If you follow up on something, you take further action about it.

theory [θíːəri] n. 추측, 가설; 이론, 학설
If you have a theory about something, you have your own opinion about it which you cannot prove but which youthink is true.

overflow [òuvərflóu] v. 넘치다, 넘쳐 흐르다; n. 넘쳐 흐름, 범람
If a liquid or a river overflows, it flows over the edges of the container or place it is in.

embarrass [imbǽrəs] v. 부끄럽게[무안하게] 하다; 어리둥절하게 하다, 당황하다
(embarrassing a. 쑥스러운)
If something or someone embarrasses you, they make you feel shy or ashamed.

recipe [résəpi] n. 조리법, 요리법
A recipe is a list of ingredients and a set of instructions that tell you how to cook something.

now that conj. ~이기 때문에
You use now or now that to indicate that an event has occurred and as a result something else may or will happen.

mention [ménʃən] vt. 말하다, 언급하다; n. 언급, 거론
If you mention something, you say something about it, usually briefly.

equipment [ikwípmənt] n. 장비, 용품
Equipment consists of the things which are used for a particular purpose, for example a hobby or job.

budget [bʌ́dʒit] n. 비용, 예산
Your budget is the amount of money that you have available to spend.

electricity [ilektrísəti] n. 전기, 전력
Electricity is a form of energy that can be carried by wires and is used for heating and lighting, and to provide power for machines.

somehow [sʌ́mhàu] ad. 여하튼, 어쨌든; 왠지, 아무래도
You use somehow to say that you do not know or cannot say how something was done or will be done.

significant [signífikənt] a. 의미심장한, 중요한
A significant action or gesture is intended to have a special meaning.

fold [fould] v. (손·팔·다리를) 끼다, 포개다; 접다, 접어 포개다
If you fold your arms or hands, you bring them together and cross or link them, for example over your chest.

make one's point idiom 생각을 밝히다, 주장이 정당함을 보여주다
If you make your point, you prove that something is true, either by arguing about it or by your actions or behavior.

glory [glɔ́:ri] n. 영광; vi. 기뻐하다, 자랑으로 여기다
Glory is the fame and admiration that you gain by doing something impressive.

measure [méʒər] v. (치수·양 등을) 측정하다, 재다; n. 계량, 측정
If you measure something out, you discover the quantity of it that you need from a larger amount.

ingredient [ingrí:diənt] n. 재료, 성분, 원료
Ingredients are the things that are used to make something, especially all the different foods you use when you are cooking a particular dish.

accidental [æ̀ksədéntl] a. 우연한; 부수적인 (accidentally ad. 우연히)
An accidental event happens by chance or as the result of an accident, and is not deliberately intended.

include [inklú:d] v. ~을 포함하다; (~에) 포함시키다
If one thing includes another thing, it has the other thing as one of its parts.

extra [ékstrə] a. 추가의; n. 추가되는 것
You use extra to describe an amount, person, or thing that is added to others of the same kind, or that can be added to others of the same kind.

nod [nad] v. (고개를) 끄덕이다, 끄덕여 나타내다; n. (고개를) 끄덕임
If you nod, you move your head downward and upward to show agreement, understanding, or approval.

quarter [kwɔ́:rtər] n. 25센트; 4분의 1; 15분
A quarter is an American or Canadian coin that is worth 25 cents.

spill [spil] v. 엎지르다, 흘리다; n. 엎지름, 유출
If a liquid spills or if you spill it, it accidentally flows over the edge of a container.

flour [flauər] n. 밀가루; 분말, 가루
Flour is a white or brown powder that is made by grinding grain, which is used to make bread, cakes, and pastry.

probably [prábəbli] ad. 아마
If you say that something is probably the case, you think that it is likely to be the case, although you are not sure.

notice [nóutis] v. ~을 의식하다; 주목하다, 관심을 기울이다; n. 신경 씀, 주목
If you notice something or someone, you become aware of them.

innocent [ínəsənt] a. 아무 잘못이 없는, 결백한; 순결한, 순진한
If someone is innocent, they did not commit a crime which they have been accused of.

exclaim [ikskléim] v. 외치다, 소리치다
If you exclaim, you say or shout something suddenly because of surprise, fear and pleasure.

set (someone) free idiom (사람·동물을) 자유롭게 하다, 석방하다
If you set someone or something free, you release or liberate them.

Chapter 10

1. What kind of detective did Buster say he was?

A. The kind that appeared in movies

B. The kind that nobody knew about

C. The kind that was shy and avoided attention

D. The kind that wanted to be recognized for his work

2. Where was Arthur when Buster came for him?

A. He was in detention.

B. He was in his homeroom class.

C. He was in the cafeteria kitchen.

D. He was in the principal's office.

3. **What did Arthur think of when he heard Miss Tingley typing?**

A. Quarters

B. Picnics

C. Crickets

D. A crowd of people

4. **What joke did the Brain make about the quarters in Mrs. MacGrady's brownies?**

A. They must have been the most expensive brownies she ever made.

B. They must have been the richest brownies she ever made.

C. They must have been the toughest brownies she ever made.

D. They must have been the hottest brownies she ever made.

5. **How did Buster feel about the mystery involving Mrs. MacGrady's missing cookies?**

A. Mrs. MacGrady would give Arthur a chance to solve this case.

B. Mrs. MacGrady could just make more cookies.

C. Mrs. MacGrady would have to solve it on her own.

D. Mrs. MacGrady should check everyone for crumbs.

Check Your Reading Speed
1분에 몇 단어를 읽는지 리딩 속도를 측정해보세요.

$$\frac{505 \text{ words}}{\text{reading time ( ) sec}} \times 60 = (\quad) \text{ WPM}$$

Build Your Vocabulary

detective [ditéktiv] n. 탐정, 형사
A detective is someone whose job is to discover what has happened in a crime or other situation and to find the people involved.

fade [feid] v. 서서히 사라지다; 바래다, 희미해지다
When something that you are looking at fades, it slowly becomes less bright or clear until it disappears.

shadow [ʃǽdou] n. 그늘, 어둠; 그림자
Shadow is darkness in a place caused by something preventing light from reaching it.

case [keis] n. 사건, 경우, 사례
A case is a crime or mystery that the police are investigating.

solve [salv] v. (수학 문제 등을) 풀다, 해결하다
If you solve a problem or a question, you find a solution or an answer to it.

reward [riwɔ́:rd] n. 보상, 보답; 현상금; v. 보답하다, 보상하다
A reward is something that you are given, for example because you have behaved well, worked hard, or provided a service to the community.

dodge [dadʒ] v. (재빨리) 피하다, 날쌔게 비키다, 몸을 홱 피하다; n. 발뺌
If you dodge, you move suddenly, often to avoid being hit, caught, or seen.

bow [bau] n. (고개 숙여 하는) 인사, 절; v. 머리를 숙이다, 절하다
When you take a bow to someone, you briefly bend your body toward them as a formal way of greeting them or showing respect.

recognize [rékəgnàiz] v. 인정하다; 알아보다, 인지하다
If someone says that they recognize something, they acknowledge that it exists or that it is true.

duck [dʌk] ① v. 피하다, 급히 움직이다; (머리나 몸을) 휙 숙이다 ② n. 오리
You say that someone ducks a duty or responsibility when you disapprove of the fact that they avoid it.

deserve [dizə́:rv] vt. ~을 할[받을] 만하다, ~할 가치가 있다
If you say that a person or thing deserves something, you mean that they should have it or receive it because of their actions or qualities.

compliment [kámpləmənt] n. 찬사, 칭찬의 말; v. 칭찬하다
A compliment is a polite remark that you say to someone to show that you like their appearance, appreciate their qualities, or approve of what they have done.

credit [krédit] n. 공적, 명예, 칭찬; 신용, 신뢰
If you get the credit for something good, people praise you because you are responsible for it, or are thought to be responsible for it.

untangle [ʌntǽŋgl] v. 복잡한 것을 풀다, 엉킨 것을 풀다
If you untangle something that is knotted or has become twisted around something, you undo the knots in it or free it.

detention [diténʃən] n. (학생에 대한 벌로서) 방과 후 남게 하기; 구금
Detention is a punishment for naughty schoolchildren, who are made to stay at school after the other children have gone home.

particular [pərtíkjulər] a. 특정한, 특별한, 특유의
You use particular to emphasize that you are talking about one thing or one kind of thing rather than other similar ones.

company [kʌ́mpəni] n. 함께 있음; (집에 온) 손님; 회사
Company is having another person or other people with you, usually when this is pleasant or stops you feeling lonely.

quarter [kwɔ́ːrtər] n. 25센트; 4분의 1; 15분
A quarter is an American or Canadian coin that is worth 25 cents.

reputation [rèpjutéiʃən] n. 평판, 명성
Something's or someone's reputation is the opinion that people have about how good they are.

in question idiom 문제가 되고 있는
If something is in question or has been called into question, doubt or uncertainty has been expressed about it and it is being discussed.

prove [pruːv] v. 입증하다, 증명하다; 드러나다, 판명되다
If you prove that something is true, you show by means of argument or evidence that it is definitely true.

innocent [ínəsənt] a. 아무 잘못이 없는, 결백한; 순결한, 순진한
If someone is innocent, they did not commit a crime which they have been accused of.

miss [mis] v. (어디에 참석하지 않아서 그 일을) 놓치다; (치거나 잡거나 닿지 못하고) 놓치다
If you miss something such as a meeting or an activity, you do not go to it or take part in it.

type [taip] v. (타자기·컴퓨터로) 타자 치다; n. 유형, 종류
If you type something, you use a typewriter or word processor to write it.

cricket [kríkit] n. 귀뚜라미
A cricket is a small jumping insect that produces short, loud sounds by rubbing its wings together.

chirp [ʧəːrp] v. 짹짹 울다; (즐거운 듯이) 말하다; n. 짹짹(새 등의 울음소리)
When a bird or an insect such as a cricket or grasshopper chirps, it makes short high-pitched sounds.

‡ unexpected [ʌnikspéktid] a. 예기치 않은, 예상 밖의
If an event or someone's behavior is unexpected, it surprises you because you did not think that it was likely to happen.

commotion [kəmóuʃən] n. 소란, 소동, 동요
A commotion is a lot of noise, confusion, and excitement.

복습 hall [hɔːl] n. (건물의) 복도, 통로; (건물 입구 안쪽의) 현관; 넓은 방[건물]
A hall in a building is a long passage with doors into rooms on both sides of it.

‡‡ advise [ædváiz] v. 충고하다, 조언하다, 권고하다
If you advise someone to do something, you tell them what you think they should do.

‡ justice [dʒʌ́stis] n. 정의, 공정; 사법, 재판
Justice is fairness in the way that people are treated.

복습 serve [sɚːrv] v. (상품·서비스·음식을) 제공하다; (어떤 기간을) 복역하다, 치르다
If something serves people or an area, it provides them with something that they need.

복습 missing [mísiŋ] a. (제자리나 집에 있지 않고) 없어진; 빠진, 누락된
If something is missing, it is not in its usual place, and you cannot find it.

end up idiom 마침내는 (~으로) 되다[가다]; 끝나다
If you end up doing something or end up in a particular state, you do that thing or get into that state even though you did not originally intend to.

‡ owe [ou] vt. 은혜를 입고 있다, 빚지고 있다
If you say that you owe a great deal to someone or something, you mean that they have helped you or influenced you a lot, and you feel very grateful to them.

peerless [píərlis] a. (뛰어나기가) 비할 데 없는
Something that is peerless is so beautiful or wonderful that you feel that nothing can equal it.

investigate [invéstəgèit] v. 수사하다, 조사하다 (investigator n. 수사관)
If someone, especially an official, investigates an event, situation, or claim, they try to find out what happened or what is the truth.

bullhorn [búllhɔːrn] n. 휴대용 확성기, 핸드 마이크; v. 확성기로 말하다
A bullhorn is a device for making your voice sound louder in the open air.

order [ɔ́ːrdər] vt. 명령을 내리다; 주문하다; n. 명령; 주문; 순서
If a person in authority orders someone to do something, they tell them to do it.

await [əwéit] v. (~을) 기다리다
Something that awaits you is going to happen or come to you in the future.

speechless [spíːʧlis] a. 말문이 막힌, 말을 못하는
If you are speechless, you are temporarily unable to speak, usually because something has shocked you.

go on idiom (잠깐 쉬었다가) 말을 계속하다; (어떤 상황이) 계속되다
If someone goes one, they continue speaking after a short pause.

plate [pleit] n. 접시, 그릇
A plate is a round or oval flat dish that is used to hold food.

aside [əsáid] ad. 한쪽으로; ~외에는
If you move something aside, you move it to one side of you.

brush [brʌʃ] v. (솔이나 손으로) 털다; 솔질하다
If you brush something off, you remove it with quick light movements of your hands.

crumb [krʌm] n. 빵 부스러기, 빵가루; 작은 조각
Crumbs are tiny pieces that fall from bread, biscuits, or cake when you cut it or eat it.

on one's own idiom 혼자서, 혼자 힘으로
If you do something on your own, you do it without any help from other people.

1장

page 5

안녕, 낯선 사람. 나는 버스터 백스터, 사설탐정이야. 짧게 버스터라고 불러도 돼. 지금부터 너에게 나의 첫 사건에 대해 말하려고 해. 그것은 내 친구 아서와 없어진 동전들, 그리고 엄청나게 많은 문제와 관련되어 있어.

모든 것은 이틀 전에 시작됐지. 평범한 수요일—화요일과 목요일 사이에 오는 바로 그 날이었어. 일주일의 중간, 어떤 일이라도 일어날 수 있는—그리고 보통 그러는 때 말이야.

학교 일과가 막 끝난 상태였습니다. 아서는 학교 복도 긴 테이블 뒤에 서 있었습니다. 그의 앞에는 25센트 동전이 반쯤 차 있는 통이 있었습니다.

page 7

"소방서가 새 강아지를 살 수 있도록 도와주세요!" 아서가 말했습니다. "25센트면 됩니다!"

몇몇 아이들이 동전을 넣었습니다.

"고맙습니다." 아서가 말했습니다. "정말 고맙습니다."

빙키 반스가 그에게 걸어왔습니다. 그의 머리와 어깨가 복도 창문으로 들어오는 빛을 막았습니다. "그 통 뭐야, 아서?"

"맥그래디 부인의 기금 모음 운동을 위해 돈을 모으고 있어. 우린 소방서를 위해 새 강아지를 살 거야." 그는 빙키에게 사진을 보여 주었습니다.

"그 개 반점이 많다. 그거 안 아픈 것이 확실해?"

"아니야, 아니야. 달마티안은 전부 이렇게 생겼어. 그래서 어떻게 생각해? 25센트 내는 거 어때?"

빙키는 고심했습니다. 그는 반짝이는 25센트 동전에 대한 생각을 작은 달마티안 강아지에 견주어 저울질했습니다. 그의 머릿속의 강아지는 구르며 작게 킁킁거리는 소리를 냈습니다. 그것은 일어나서 꼬리를 흔들었습니다. 25센트 동전은 단지 가만히 빛나고만 있었습니다.

page 8

"여기." 빙키가 말했습니다. 그는 주머니에 손을 넣고 25센트 동전을 꺼내 통 안에 튕겨 넣었습니다. "그런데 한 가지만." 그가 아서를 노려보며 덧붙였습니다.

"뭔데?"

"누구에게도 내가 줬다고 말하지 마. 내 이미지에 좋지 않아."

"알겠어." 아서가 말했습니다.

빙키는 잠시나마 만족해 보였습니다.

"이봐, 아서!" 버스터가 복도를 달려오며 소리 질렀습니다.

"그 멍청한 모자는 뭐야?" 아서가 물었습니다.

"이 모자 멍청하지 않아." 버스터가 말했습니다. "이건 페도라야—내 새로운 탐정 세트의 일부지. 난 기웃거리고—아, 범죄를 찾고 있었어."

page 9

"뭔가를 좀 찾았니?"

"아니." 버스터는 모자의 챙을 뒤로 밀었습니다. "하지만 난 비밀 정보를 좀 얻었어."

그는 좌우를 주의해서 보며, 아무도 듣고 있지 않다는 것을 확인했습니다.

"너 이걸 다른 사람한테 새어나가게 하지 않겠다고 약속해?"

아서가 고개를 끄덕였습니다.

버스터가 몸을 앞으로 숙였습니다. "3학년 소풍이 이번 주 금요일이야." 그는 속삭였습니다.

아서는 어이가 없어서 눈을 굴렸습니다. "그건 나도 알아, 버스터. 2주 동안 안내문이 붙어 있었잖아."

"오. 뭐, 내가 반은 맞았네. 그래도 여전히 정보잖아. 어쨌든, 난 포기하지 않을 거야. 난 범죄를 찾을 거야. 어쩌면 오락실에서 찾을지도 모르지. 우리 엄마가 오늘 오후에 날 데려다 준다고 했어. 너도 오고 싶니?"

대부분의 아이들이 집에 돌아간 것 같았습니다. 아서는 아마도 오늘 모을 수 있는 모든 동전을 모았다고 판단했습니다. 그리고 오락실은 멋진 곳이었습니다.

page 10

"물론이지." 그가 말했습니다. "잠깐 내가 맥그래디 부인께 이 동전들만 전해 드리고."

그는 통에 담긴 동전들을 종이가방 안으로 비워 담았습니다.

"난 나가서 엄마를 찾을게." 버스터가 말했습니다. "널 기다리고 있을게. 서둘러!"

아서는 고개를 끄덕이고 복도를 뛰어갔습니다.

2장

page 11

나는 그 후 몇 분 동안 아서와 같이 있지 않았어. 아마 내가 같이 있었다면, 그는 아무런 문제도 없었을 거야. 하지만 탐정의 안내서에서 말하는 것처럼, 인생이 잘못된 방향으로 가려고 할 때는, 단지 길을 잃지 않으려고 노력해야 해.

아서는 서둘러서 식당 부엌으로 갔습니다. 그는 수위 아저씨 모리스 씨가 점심시간 이후에 바닥을 치워두었다는 것을 알았습니다. "위에 놓고 먹을 수 있을 만큼 깨끗하지." 모리스 씨는 이렇게 말하곤 했지만, 아서는 접시를 더 선호했습니다.

맥그래디 부인은 통화중이었습니다.

page 12

"뭐라고요, 소장님? 아직 이름을 생각해 보지 않았다구요?"

아서는 그녀의 관심을 끌려고 손짓했습니다. 그는 버스터와 그의 어머니를 기다리게 하고 싶지 않았습니다.

하지만 맥그래디 부인은 그를 보지 못했습니다.

"스모키. 네, 개 이름으로 좋네요. 알겠어요, 알겠어요..."

아서는 인내심을 가지려고 했습니다. 그의 옆에 있는 조리대에는 제빵 재료들이 있었습니다. 밀가루와 설탕 봉투, 버터 조각, 계란, 그리고 초콜릿 조각들이 있었습니다.

"스모키가 있는 곳에는, 소방대원이 있다. 귀엽네요, 소장님. 아주 귀여워요. 전 그냥 개가 콤플렉스를 가지지 않으면 좋겠어요. 개들은 매우 예민해요, 아시잖아요."

아서의 손에 있는 가방이 점점 무거워졌습니다. 그는 내려놓으려고 가다가 실수로 밀가루 봉투를 넘어뜨렸습니다.

"체스터도 개 이름으로 좋아요. 그렇게 생각하지 않으세요? 제 첫 번째 남편 이름이 체스터였어요."

page 14

맥그래디 부인이 여전히 보고 있지 않은 덕분에, 아서는 그녀가 그를 보지 않은 채로 밀가루를 치울 수 있었습니다. 밀가루의 일부는 동전이 들어 있는 가방으로 들어갔지만, 밀가루가 동전에 어떤 해도 끼치지 않을 것이기 때문에 그건 괜찮았습니다.

아서는 시계를 보았습니다. 그는 그곳에 5분이 넘도록 서 있었습니다.

"맥그래디 부인? 실례합니다, 맥그래디 부인?" 그는 동전 가방을 들었습니다.

그녀는 손을 흔들었지만, 그녀가 아서에게 손짓을 하는 것인지 아니면 전화를 하면서 움직이는 것인지 알기가 힘들었습니다.

"저 이만 갈게요—" 아서가 말하기 시작했습니다.

하지만 맥그래디 부인은 여전히 통화를 하면서 돌아서 있었습니다.

아서는 더 이상 기다릴 수 없었습니다. 만약 그가 그런다면, 버스터는 발끈할지도 모릅니다. 맥그래디 부인은 어쨌든 곧 전화를 끊을 것이었습니다.

"저 가방을 조리대 위에 둘게요." 아서가 외쳤습니다. "바로 여기요, 밀가루 옆에요."

page 15

그리고 그는 떠났습니다.

3장

page 16

아서와 내가 오락실에 도착했을 때, 내 마음 속에는 두 가지가 있었어. 하나는 게임 그 자체에 관한 것이었지. 난 지난번에 나를 성질나게 한 외계인 탐험가의 복수전을 원했어. 그 게임은 한 수 가르침 받을 필요가 있었어. 그리고 내가 그것을 할 적임자였지.

내 마음 속에 있던 다른 하나는 해결할 미스터리를 찾는 것이었어. 오락실은 쓰레기통이 파리를 끄는 것처럼 수상한 인물들을 당기는 구석이 있거든. 내가 계속 경계하고 있다면 무언가가 내 앞에 나타날 것이라고 생각했어.

page 17

"버스터," 아서가 말했습니다. "너 그 확대경 가지고 뭐하니?"

"그냥 조사하고 있어." 버스터는 테이블을 가까이 들여다보고 있었습니다. "어떤 미스터리는 숨바꼭질하는 것을 좋아하거든." 그는 위아래로 살펴보면서 확대경을 다시 아서에게로 옮겼습니다. "예를 들어, 너를 봐."

"내가 어때서?" 아서가 말했습니다.

"네 옷에 하얀 것이 묻었어."

"아니야."

버스터는 더 가까이 보았습니다. "확실히 가루 같은 거야."

아서는 내려다보았습니다. 뭔가가 조금... 갑자기 그는 미소를 지었습니다. "오, 그건 미스터리가 아니야. 식당에 동전을 갖다 놓을 때, 내가 실수로 밀가루를 쏟았어. 그게 내 셔츠 위에도 묻은 것이 틀림없어."

버스터는 실망스러워 보였습니다. "뭐, 그건 미스터리가 될 수도 있었네."

page 19

"미안." 아서가 말했습니다. "아무튼, 난 우리가 여기에 게임하러 온 줄 알았는데."

그들은, 스스로 게임하기도 하고 다른 사람이 하는 것을 보기도 하면서, 여기저기 돌아다녔습니다. 둘 중 누구도 크래쉬코스 2000에서 살아남거나 유령 호텔에서 하룻밤을 다 보낼 정도로 운이 좋지는 않았지만, 버스터는 외계인 탐험가에서는 더 잘했습니다.

"맛 좀 봐라, 이 더러운 돌연변이야!" 그는 외쳤습니다. "아, 복수는 달콤해!" 이전에는 돌연변이가 항상 그에게 했던 일이었습니다.

"앞으로 몇 분만 더 줄게, 얘들아." 버스터의 엄마가 그들에게 외쳤습니다. 그녀는 그들을 오락실 밖에서 기다리고 있었습니다.

버스터는 돈이 다 떨어졌지만, 아서는 여전히 한 게임을 더 할 수 있을 만큼 충분히 가지고 있었습니다. 그는 핀볼

게임을 하기로 결정했습니다. 그는 그의 25센트 동전을 넣고 손잡이를 당겼습니다. 그가 그것을 놓자, 공이 구멍 위로 발사되어 경사로 주변을 돌았습니다.

page 20

"잘해, 아서, 아자!" 핀볼에는 그다지 운이 따르지 않았던 버스터가 말했습니다.

공은 플랫폼을 돌며 튕겨 나갔습니다. 그것이 속도를 잃고 아래로 떨어질 때마다, 아서는 집게손으로 그것을 잡아 다시 위로 보냈습니다.

"와! 큰일 날 뻔 했어, 아서! 계속 올려!"

아서의 점수가 오르자, 기계는 더욱 더 많은 색으로 번쩍였습니다. 관중들이 그의 뒤에 모이기 시작했습니다.

"거기, 조심해!"

"기다려... 지금이야!"

아서는 승승장구 하고 있었습니다.

"스피너를 잡아!"

아서는 최선을 다했지만, 마침내 세 번째 공이 오른쪽 집게손을 재빨리 피하며 구멍 안으로 빠졌습니다.

page 21

"아서, 네가 해냈어!" 버스터가 외쳤습니다. "네가 최고 점수를 기록했어!"

아서가 올려다보았습니다. 그의 868,233점이 첫 번째 자리에 있었습니다. 그는 심지어 그 점수 옆에 이름의 첫 글자를 입력하게 됐습니다.

"저 점수는 영원히 남을 거야." 버스터가 말했습니다. 구경꾼들이 환호하자 그는 아서의 등을 두드렸습니다.

그들이 오락실을 떠날 때, 버스터는 여전히 흥분해 있었습니다. "내 가장 친한 친구가 최고점을 기록했어요." 그는 모두에게 자랑스럽게 말했습니다.

그것은 해결해야 할 미스터리를 찾는 것과는 달랐지만, 여전히 그건 꽤 좋았습니다.

4장

page 22

내가 인정하고 싶지 않은 만큼, 나는 약간 우울해지기 시작했어. 조사해야 할 미스터리를 찾는 것이 왜 그렇게 어려운 것이지? 모든 탐정들이 이런 문제를 가지고 있었나? 그래도 나는 최소한 공유할 만한 좋은 소식을 다음날 학교에서 얻었지.

"옆으로 물러나, 모두들. 길을 비켜! 핀볼의 천재가 지나가신다."

버스터는 그와 아서가 복도를 따라 걸어갈 때 이런 말들을 했습니다.

"버스터, 제발!" 아서가 말했습니다. "창피해."

"겸손할 필요 없어, 아서. 넌 주목받을 자격이 있어."

아서는 한숨을 쉬었습니다.

"민첩한 손가락이 여기 있소! 매와 같은 눈. 고양이 같은 반사 신경!"

그들이 교장실을 지나갈 때, 하니 교장 선생님이 그들에게 들어오라고 손짓했습니다.

"좋은 아침이구나, 아서, 버스터." 그가 말했습니다. "오, 아서, 맥그래디 부인에게 네가 그녀의 모금 운동을 위해 모은 동전들을 전하는 걸 잊지 말거라."

"저 이미 그랬는데요, 하니 선생님."

학교 비서인 팅글리 씨가 얼굴을 찌푸렸습니다. "그거 이상한데요. 맥그래디 부인은 절대 받지 않았다고 하던데요."

"아하!" 버스터가 말했습니다. "아마도 도둑맞았나 봐요."

"버스터, 제발 가만히 있으렴." 하니 선생님이 말했습니다. 교장 선생님은 아서에게 몸을 돌렸습니다. "네가 혹시 실수로 집에 가져갔을 수 있잖니?"

"아니요." 버스터가 말했습니다. "얘는 곧장 저랑 오락실에 갔어요. 사실, 앤 핀볼을 엄청 잘했어요. 여러분께서는 지금 미스터 득점왕을 보고 계십니다."

"정말?" 하니 선생님은 얼굴을 찌푸렸습니다. 팅글리 씨도 얼굴을 찌푸렸습니다.

"저도 한 번 높은 점수를 받았었어요." 버스터가 계속했습니다. "엄청나게 돈이 들었죠. 생일선물로 받은 돈을 다 썼어요. 25센트 동전 백 개 정도요. 맙소사, 정말 내가—"

버스터는 갑자기 멈추었습니다. 그는 아서를 쳐다보았습니다. 하니 선생님과 팅글리 씨도 그랬습니다.

"무슨 문제 있어요?" 아서가 물었습니다.

"우리가 여기 작은 미스터리를 가지고 있구나." 하니 선생님이 말했습니다.

팅글리 씨가 다시 얼굴을 찌푸렸습니다. "그렇게 작지 않아요." 그녀가 말했습니다.

잠시 후, 아서는 교장실에 앉아 있는 자신을 발견했습니다. 그는 자신이 매우 작게 느껴졌습니다. 그가 앉아 있는 의자는 매우 불편하게 느껴졌습니다.

"너는 그 돈에 대해 책임을 져야 한단다." 하니 선생님이 말하고 있었습니다.

"당연히 네가 그래야지." 팅글리 씨가 덧붙였습니다.

아서는 의자로 더욱 움츠러들었습니다.

그는 근엄한 얼굴들을 번갈아 보았습니다. "그러니까... 선생님은 *제가* 그 동전들을 훔쳤다고 생각하세요? 하지만 저는 그걸 식당 조리대에 놓고 왔어요."

"글쎄, 맥그래디 부인은 그것을 전혀 보지 못했다고 하는구나." 하니 선생님이 말했습니다. "네가 그것에 대한 책임이 있단다. 그리고 만약 돈이 나오지 않으면, 미안하지만 너는 하루를—"

팅글리 씨가 헛기침을 했습니다.

"내 말은, 일주일 동안 방과 후에 남아야 한단다." 하니 선생님은 잠시 멈추었습니다. "그리고 내일 있을 3학년 소풍도 못 갈 거야."

아서는 겁에 질렸습니다.

그가 교장실을 나올 때, 버스터가 그에게 달려 왔습니다.

"그래, 어떻게 됐어?"

아서는 그에게 설명했습니다. "내가 처음으로 맡은 중요한 일인데, 모두가 나를 도둑이라고 생각해. 하지만 나는 결백해."

page 27

"물론 너는 그렇지." 버스터가 말했습니다. "그게 너한테 탐정이 필요한 이유야. 예를 들어... 나 같은."

"난 모르겠어, 버스터. 너 정말 그 동전들에게 무슨 일이 일어났는지 알아낼 수 있을 것 같아?"

"문제없어! 난 이 사건을 자면서도 풀수 있어. 아, 아니지, 깨어있어야 하겠지. 잠옷도 입지 않은 채로 말이야. 하지만 걱정하지 마, 아서. 버스터 백스터가 이 사건을 맡았어. 넌 내일 소풍을 가게 될 거야. 나를 믿어."

아서는 그를 믿고 싶었지만, 좀 더 희망적으로 느껴지길 바랐습니다. "좋아, 버스터, 네 일을 해. 하지만 나한테 하나만 약속해."

"물론이지. 뭔데?"

"나를 더 심각한 문제에 빠뜨리지 않도록 해줘. 지금 이 상태로도 충분히 나쁜 상황이니까."

5장

page 28

모든 사건에는 주요 목격자가 있고, 이번 사건도 다르지 않아. 나는 그녀가 누구인지 알고 있고, 그녀 역시 그녀가 누구인지 알고 있지.

성: 맥그래디.

이름: 부인.

직업: 식당 아줌마.

버스터는 맥그래디 부인을 식당 부엌에서 발견했습니다. 그녀는 큰 그릇에 담긴 재료들을 섞고 있었습니다. 그는 그가 아서의 없어진 동전들을 수사하고 있다고 설명했습니다.

page 29

"어제 오후 당신의 행방에 대해서 제게 말씀해 주시겠어요?"

"'행방'이라고? 내가 어디 있었는지 묻는 것 치고는 꽤 격조 있는 방법이구나. 음, 나는 바로 여기 부엌에 있었단다. 브라우니를 만들면서 말이지. 버스터, 네 손을 그 그릇에서 떼어 놓으렴!"

"아하!" 버스터가 그의 손을 뒤로 빼며 말했습니다. "아마도 제가 이걸 맛봐야겠어요. 이게 증거가 될 수도 있거든요."

맥그래디 부인은 그에게 주걱을 흔들었습니다. "좋은 시도야. 하지만 넌 다른 아이들처럼 소풍날까지 기다려야 해."

그녀는 작은 체리 타르트들로 덮여 있는 긴 테이블 쪽으로 옮겨 가서는 각각의 위에 휘핑크림을 짜기 시작했습니다.

"소장님하고 통화한 것이 기억나는구나. 우리는 꽤 긴 대화를 했지. 그러고 나서 난 브라우니를 만들었어."

page 30

"아서를 보았나요?"

"아니, 오후 내내 아무도 보지 못했어. 오, 잠깐, 그렇지 않아. 모리스 씨가 여기 있었어. 내 반죽기가 몇 번 고장 나서, 브라우니 반죽이 바닥으로 넘쳤어. 그가 그 난장판을 닦으려고 왔었지."

"흠." 버스터가 체리 타르트 하나를 입안으로 넣으며 말했습니다.

"너 아마도 모리스 씨랑 이야기를 하는 게 어떠니." 맥그래디 부인이 제안했습니다.

"암쇄합니다." 버스터가 중얼거리고는, 그녀가 뭐라고 말하기도 전에 뛰어 나갔습니다.

그는 학교 수위 아저씨 모리스 씨가 복도를 따라 수레를 밀고 있는 것을 발견했습니다.

"실례합니다, 모리스 씨." 버스터가 말했습니다. "제가 몇 가지 질문을 해도 괜찮을까요?"

"말해보렴."

page 32

버스터는 그가 어제 오후부터 있었던 일련의 사건들을 재구성하고 있다고 설명했습니다.

"'일련의 사건들'이라고?" 모리스 씨가 말했습니다. "너 TV에 나오는 탐정처럼 얘기하는구나."

"정말요?" 버스터가 말했습니다. 그는 활짝 웃었습니다. 그러고 나서 그는 탐정들이 활짝 웃지 않는다는 것을 기억하고 다시 심각하게 보이려고 노력했습니다.

"어제 일을 말씀해 주세요."

"음, 어디 보자." 모리스 씨가 말했습니다. "나는 교무실에 있었는데—"

"아하!" 버스터가 의심스럽다는 듯이

말했습니다. "그리고 거기서 뭘 하고 계셨나요?"

"전등을 갈아 끼웠어. 그리고 부엌에 와 달라는 전화를 받았지. 맥그래디 부인이 그녀의 반죽기에 문제가 생긴 것 같더라고. 내가 거기 갔을 땐, 바닥이 브라우니 반죽으로 다 덮여 있었어. 그래서 내가 그 난장판을 치웠지."

버스터는 팔짱을 꼈습니다. "항상 맥그래디 부인의 뒤처리를 하시나요?"

page 33

"아니, 자주는 아니야. 그녀는 대체적으로 꽤 깔끔하지. 하지만 난 도와줄 수 있어서 기뻤단다. 또 질문이 있니?"

버스터는 질문을 더 생각해 내고 싶었습니다. 그는 질문하는 것이 좋았습니다. 하지만 그는 더 이상 생각해 낼 수 없었습니다.

"지금으로선 없어요. 하지만 부탁 하나만 들어주세요. 마을을 떠나지 마세요."

모리스 씨는 미소를 지었습니다. "뭐든지 네 말대로 하마, 버스터."

그는 그의 양동이와 대걸레를 모아 걸어가기 시작했습니다. 그가 한 발 한 발 걸을 때마다 짤랑하는 소리가 났습니다.

"잠시만요, 모리스 씨!" 버스터가 그를 잡기 위해 뛰어왔습니다. "그 짤랑하는 소리... 동전처럼 들리는데요! 아주 많은 동전!"

모리스 씨는 그의 주머니에서 열쇠들로 가득한 큰 열쇠꾸러미를 꺼냈습니다. "네가 무슨 말하는지 알아." 그가 짤랑하는 소리를 내며 말했습니다. "나도 자주 그런 생각을 한단다."

page 34

"오. 그럼, 괜찮아요, 이제."

사실 괜찮지 않다고 버스터는 생각했습니다. 적어도 아서에게는 말입니다. 그는 빨리 사건의 진상을 밝히길 바라고 있었습니다. 하지만 그가 파헤치면 파헤칠수록, 사건은 더욱 복잡해졌습니다.

그리고 그 진상은 어디에도 보이지 않았습니다.

6장

page 35

나는 몇 시간 동안 그 사건에 매달려 있었지만, 체리 타르트 하나를 제외하고는, 그 일에 대해 보여줄 만한 성과가 거의 없었어. 누구도 용의자를 거짓말쟁이라고 부르지 않았지만, 마찬가지로 누구도 그의 이야기를 옹호하지 않았지. 나는 현장의 변화가 도움이 될 거라고 생각해서, 용의자의 집으로 향했어. 그곳에서 나는 용의자의 여동생을 만났어.

그녀는 꽤 뻔뻔한 녀석처럼 보였지만, 나는 내가 그녀를 다룰 수 있다는 걸 알았지.

"이봐, D.W., 넌 뭔가를 알고 있는 게 틀림없어."

그들은 리드 씨네 부엌에 서 있었습니다. 아서는 잠시 나간 상태라고 D.W.가 말했었습니다. 하지만 오빠는 멀리 가지는 못했을 거야, 라고 그녀는 생각했습니다. 경찰이 아마도 기차와 버스정류장을 지키고 있을 것입니다. "그리고 아마 지금쯤 오빠 사진이 현상수배범 포스터에 붙었겠지." 그녀가 말했습니다.

page 36

"D.W., 나는 아서의 혐의를 벗기려고 하고 있지, 그를 감옥으로 보내려는 게 아니야. 이제 잘 생각해 봐."

D.W.가 얼굴을 찌푸렸습니다. "알겠어, 알겠어, 내가 아는 걸 말해 줄게."

"계속해." 버스터가 그의 메모장과 연필을 꺼냈습니다.

"준비됐어? 좋아, 이걸 적어. 한 글자도 빠트리지 말고."

버스터가 고개를 끄덕였습니다.

"그... 모자... 너한테... 멍청해... 보여."

버스터는 연필을 내려놓았습니다. "이거 심각하다고, D.W. 게다가, 난 이 모자 좋아해."

D.W.가 킬킬거렸습니다.

"이제 주제로 돌아가서—"

page 38

"이게 뭐야, 버스터, 심문이라도 하는 거야? 만약 내가 뭔가를 안다면, 나는 물론 말하겠지... 뭐, 아마도 너한테는 아니고. 다른 사람에게 말이야."

버스터는 그의 페도라를 밀어 올렸습니다. "나한테 연막작전 같은 것을 하려고 하지 마. 난 너를 창문 너머로 보듯이 다 꿰뚫어 볼 수 있어. 이제, 다시 어제 일에 대해서 생각해 봐. 아서가 짤랑거리는 큰 주머니를 가져오지 않았니... 알잖아, 다른 데 정신이 팔려서 실수로 말이야?"

D.W.는 그를 노려보았습니다. "버스터, 너 지금 내 오빠에 대해 말하고 있어! 오빠는 절대 다른 사람의 돈을 가져다가 그렇게 집으로 가져오거나 하지 않아."

"진정해, D.W. 난 아서가 일부러 나쁜 일을 했다고 생각하지 않아. 하지만 그가 깜빡 잊었던 것일 수도 있잖아. 난 그저 모든 가능성을 확인해 보는 거야."

"아서는 그렇게 멍청하지 않아." D.W.가 계속했습니다. 명백하게도, 그녀는 이 문제에 대해 심각하게 생각해 봤던 것 같습니다. "그는 절대 그냥 돈을 집에 가져오지 않았을 거야. 너무 많은 질문에 답해야 하잖아. 너무 많은 사람들이 그걸 봤을 거고. 하지만 그는 그 것이 근처에 있기를 바랐겠지. 숨겨져서. 안전하게. 하지만 어디에? 내가 생각해 낼 수 없는 게 그거야. 아서는 그렇게 똑똑하다는 것은 아니야. 하지만 그래도..."

page 39

그녀는 머리를 긁었습니다.

"그렇구나!" 그녀는 외쳤습니다. "우리는 최근에 파헤친 흔적이 있는지 잔디밭을 조사해야 해!"

"하지만 D.W.—"

그녀는 문밖으로 뛰어나갔습니다. 하지만 버스터가 그녀를 따라가기 전에, 아서가 걸어 들어왔습니다.

"오, 버스터! 네가 여기 있다니 기뻐. 이건 좋은 소식을 뜻하겠지?"

"미안, 아서. 사건은 아직 종결되지 않았어."

아서는 한숨을 쉬었습니다.

"난 그저 철저하려고 노력하고 있어." 버스터가 설명했습니다. "탐정은 철저할 필요가 있어."

"버스터, 만약 네가 누가 그랬는지 내일까지 밝혀내지 못하면, 난 소풍을 못 가게 될 거야."

"알아. 난 아직—"

그는 D.W.가 삽을 들고 지나가자 주저했습니다.

page 40

"실례할게. 옆으로 비켜. 지나간다."

아서는 D.W.를 바라보고 뭔가 말하기 시작했지만, 버스터가 손을 들었습니다.

"너 묻지 않는 것이 좋을 거야." 그가 말했습니다. "넌 정말 알고 싶지 않을 거야."

7장

page 41

상황은 좋아 보이지 않았어. 여전히 모든 정황이 여전히 단 한 사람—아서를 지목하고 있었어. 그가 정말 범죄를 계획한 사람일까? 나는 그가 비밀 은신처에서, 빛나는 25센트 동전의 바닷속을 헤엄치고 있는 것을 머릿속에 그려 보려고 했어. 그가 미친 듯이 웃을 때 동전들이 그의 손가락 사이로 빠져 나가는 거야. 25센트! 25센트! 그는 절대 만족할 수 없어.

그날 저녁 백스터 씨네 저녁식사는 조용했습니다. 백스터 부인은 버스터가 그의 하루에 대해 전부 말하는 것에 익숙했습니다. 하지만 오늘 밤엔 버스터가 조용했습니다. 너무 조용했습니다.

page 42

"너 괜찮니?" 엄마가 물었습니다.

버스터는 고개를 끄덕였습니다.

"하지만 너 디저트를 두 그릇밖에 안 먹었잖니. 그건 너답지 않아, 버스터. 너 정말로 머리가 아프거나 열이 있는 건 아니지?"

버스터는 고개를 저었습니다. "이 사건 때문이에요, 엄마. 난 어떻게 아서를 도울지 아직 생각해 내지 못했어요."

"넌 좋은 친구야, 버스터. 난 아서가 그걸 고마워할 거라고 확신해."

"저도 그러면 좋겠어요." 하지만 지금 당장 아서에게는 좋은 친구 그 이상이 필요해요, 라고 버스터는 생각했습니다. 그는 좋은 탐정이 필요했습니다.

나중에, 버스터는 메모장을 뒤적거리며 그의 책상에 앉았습니다. 그는 단서들을, 그가 사건을 해결하도록 도울 어떤 단서라도, 찾고 있었습니다. 그는 까다롭게 느끼지도 않았습니다. 큰 단서든, 작은 단서든, 누더기 같은 단서든— 버스터는 어떤 것이든 기꺼이 받아들였을 것입니다.

page 43

전화가 울렸습니다.

"버스터, 너한테 온 전화다."

브레인이었습니다. 그는 버스터에게 운이 따르고 있는지 궁금해 했습니다.

"아직 아니야." 버스터가 알렸습니다.

"뭐, 계속 시도해 봐. 뭐가 생각나면, 내가 다시 전화할게."

몇 분 뒤, 전화가 다시 울렸습니다. 이번에는 프랜신이었습니다.

"진전이 있니?" 그녀가 물었습니다.

"아니." 버스터가 말했습니다.

"알겠어. 나한테 계속 알려줘."

그가 수화기를 내려놓으려는 찰나에 전화가 다시 울렸습니다. 이번에는 머피가 전화했습니다. "우리가 단서를 살 수 없다는 게 아쉬워." 그녀가 말했습니다. "그게 상황을 훨씬 쉽게 만들 텐데."

버스터는 동의했습니다. 하지만 단서는 파는 것이 아니었습니다.

그 후에는 전화기는 조용했습니다. 버스터는 침대에 누웠고 소용돌이치는 이미지들이—맥그래디 부인, 모리스 씨, 그리고 아서가—그의 마음속에서 지나갔습니다. 그들은 모두 어느 정도 관계되어 있었습니다. 그는 단지 퍼즐 조각들을 맞추기만 하면 되었습니다.

page 44

"버스터, 시간이 늦었다!"

"난 지금 사건을 풀고 있어요."

"글쎄, 넌 자야해, 탐정 씨. 넌 로봇이 아니잖니."

"맞아요, 나는..." 버스터는 껑충 뛰어 두 발로 벌떡 일어섰습니다. "로봇! 그거에요! 엄마, 사랑해요!"

그는 전화기로 가서 아서에게 전화를 걸었습니다.

"여보세요?" 아서가 말했습니다.

"좋은 소식이야!" 버스터가 소리 질렀습니다. "내가 그걸 알아냈어!"

"정말?" 아서는 흥분했습니다. "말해 봐!"

"좋아. 그러니까, 동전들은 악당 로봇 부대에게 도둑맞은 거야. 그들은 연료로 금속이 필요해. 아무도 그들을 눈치채지 못한 거지. 왜냐하면 그들이 스스로 모습을 바꿀 수 있으니까... 어떤 모양으로든 말이야..."

page 46

아서는 한숨 쉬었습니다. "그게 다야? 그게 너의 대발견이야?"

"이런, 조금 전에는 훨씬 괜찮게 들렸는데..."

"너 잠 좀 자야겠다." 아서가 말했습니다.

"알겠어." 버스터가 말했습니다. "너도."

"노력할게." 아서가 말했습니다. 하지만 그의 유일한 기회가 로봇 부대를 찾는 것에 달려 있다면, 그는 긴 밤을 보내게 될 것이라고 생각했습니다.

8장

page 47

탐정들은 강인해야 하지만, 그들 역시 친구가 아파할 때엔 고통을 느껴. 그리고 그건 나에게도 다르지 않아. 나는 아서의 눈에서 그가 행복하지 않다는 것을 알 수 있었어. 사실, 그의 입, 처진 어깨, 심지어 그의 귀에서도 알 수 있었어. 아서는 엉망이었어.

"너 정말 나랑 같이 있는 게 눈에 띄어도 괜찮겠어?" 아서는 다음날 아침 학교 가는 길에 물었습니다.

"물론이지." 버스터가 말했습니다.

"사람들이 너를 범죄의 동료라고 생각하기 시작할 거야. 넌 나의 공범, 나의 심복, 나의—"

page 48

"아서, 그만해! 들어 봐, 나는 절대 너를 버리지 않아. 나는 가라앉는 배를 버리는 쥐새끼 같은 사람이 아니라고. 이런, 만약 네가 감옥에 간다고 해도, 나는 너한테 편지 쓸 거야. 나는 너를 보러갈 거고. 뭐, 너도 알겠지만..."

버스터는 이것이 그다지 도움이 되고 있지 않다는 것을 깨달았습니다. "어쨌든," 그가 덧붙였습니다. "난 네가 오늘 소풍을 가지 못해서 정말 유감스러워. 그리고 이건 내가 나쁜 탐정이라서 그래. 난 네가 결백하다는 것을 알아."

아서는 미소 지으려고 노력했습니다. "고마워, 버스터."

"난 너를 실망시키고 싶지 않아. 나한테 조금 더 시간이 있었다면."

"잊어버려." 아서가 말했습니다. "넌 최선을 다했어. 너는 형편없는 탐정일 수는 있어도—"

"나쁜, 아서. 난 *나쁜* 탐정이라고 했어."

"오, 알겠어. 너는 나쁜 탐정일 수는 있어도, 여전히 나의 좋은 친구야."

page 49

버스터와 아서는 곧 학교에 도착했습니다. 버스터는 다른 아이들과 함께 소풍 버스를 타는 줄에 섰습니다.

랫번 선생님이 아서에게 손짓으로 신호했습니다.

"이렇게 돼서 유감이다, 아서."

"저도요, 랫번 선생님."

선생님이 고개를 끄덕였습니다. "포기하지 마. 나는 진실은 결국엔 밝혀질 것이라고 믿는다."

아서도 물론 그렇게 바랐습니다.

"학생들!" 하니 교장 선생님이 확성기에 대고 소리 질렀습니다. "모두 이제 버스에 타세요."

버스터는 빙키와 브레인과 함께 서 있었습니다. 그들은 앞으로 움직이기 시작했습니다.

"불쌍한 아서." 브레인이 말했습니다.

"좋은 변호사가 그가 처벌을 면하게 해줄 거야." 빙키가 말했습니다. "그들은 항상 그렇게 하거든."

"하지만 아서는 결백해." 버스터가 말했습니다. "난 단지 그것을 어떻게 증명할지 모를 뿐이야. 답은 바로 내 앞 어딘가에 있어. 이봐, 그거 뭐야?"

page 51

그는 빙키의 셔츠를 가리켰습니다.

빙키는 내려다보았습니다. "설탕 가루일 거야, 아마. 나 학교 오는 길에 도넛을 먹었거든."

"오. 봐, 그런 게 증거야. 만약 이게 없어진 도넛에 관한 사건이었다면, 나는 다 준비되어 있는 거지." 버스터는 얼굴을 찌푸렸습니다. "난 이제 더 이상 똑바로 생각할 수 없어."

"난 네가 어떤 기분인지 알아." 브레인이 말했습니다. "가끔씩 내가 어려운 수학 문제를 풀 때, 나는 내 머리가 정보들로 넘치는 것 같이 느껴."

"계속 움직이세요." 하니 선생님이 말했습니다.

버스터는 버스에 올랐습니다. 갑자기 그가 멈추더니 브레인을 쳐다보았습니다.

"넘친다고? 넘쳐!"

"압박감이 그를 괴롭히나 봐." 빙키가 속삭였습니다.

page 52

"그거야!" 버스터가 외쳤습니다. 그는 브레인의 손을 잡고 흔들었습니다. "그거야!"

"뭐가 그건데?" 브레인이 말했습니

다.

버스터는 질주하듯 버스에서 내려 하니 선생님과 거의 부딪힐 뻔했습니다.

"거기서 멈춰라, 버스터. 넌 잘못된 방향으로 가고 있어."

"하니 선생님! 저 그 사건을 풀었어요. 어서 오세요!"

대답을 기다릴 틈도 없이, 그는 학교 안으로 앞장서 갔습니다.

9장

page 53

모든 탐정들은 언제나 냉정하고, 침착하고, 태연하길 바라지. 그리고 나도 다를 바 없어. 하지만 그건 사무실에서 발을 책상 위에 올려놓고 등을 기대 편안하게 앉아 있을 때에나 쉽게 할 수 있는 말이야. 네가 죽음보다 더 심각한 운명에 처한 너의 가장 친한 친구를 구했을 때에는 이야기가 완전 다르지.

부엌에서, 맥그래디 부인은 학교 소풍을 위해 짐을 꾸리고 있었습니다. 그녀는 샌드위치, 감자칩, 그리고 주스 통들을 깔끔하게 조리대 위에 정리해 놓았습니다.

그녀가 브라우니 한 판을 사각형으로 자를 준비를 하고 있을 때 버스터가

서둘러 들어왔습니다. 그는 뒤에 하니 선생님을 끌고 오고 있었습니다. "천천히, 버스터." 하니 선생님이 말했습니다. "과속으로 체포당하고 싶지는 않구나."

page 55

맥그래디 부인은 놀란 것처럼 보였습니다. "버스터! 하니 선생님! 여기서 뭐하세요?"

하니 선생님은 목청을 가다듬었습니다. "가설을 하나 확인하려고 따라왔어요. 계속하렴, 버스터."

"맥그래디 부인, 왜 브라우니 반죽이 넘쳤는지 아세요?"

"잘 모르겠는데. 그건 좀 당황스러웠다고 말할 수는 있겠구나. 하지만 모리스 씨가 친절하게 청소하는 걸 도와주셨지."

"그런 일이 전에도 있었나요? 넘치는 것 말이에요, 제 말은."

"아니. 나는 항상 주의한단다. 하지만 이번에는 내가 너무 많이 만들었나 봐."

"다른 조리법을 사용했나요?"

맥그래디 부인은 잠시 멈추고 생각했습니다. "글쎄, 아니, 네가 이제 언급하니까 말인데. 조리법은 평소와 똑같았어."

page 56

"새로운 기구를 사용했나요?"

맥그래디 부인이 웃었습니다. "내 예산으로는 안 된단다. 나한테 전기를 주

는 것만으로도 다행이지."

하니 선생님은 헛기침을 했습니다.

버스터는 칼을 들어 브라우니 틀에서 사각형으로 한 조각을 잘라냈습니다.

"그런데 어쨌든 무슨 일이 생겼어요. 이전엔 일어나지 않았었던 일이 말이에요. 중요한 의미가 있다고 생각하지 않으세요?"

하니 선생님은 팔짱을 꼈습니다. "버스터, 네 요점을 말해라, 제발. 버스가 기다리고 있어."

버스터는 거의 다 왔습니다. 하지만 탐정들은 그들의 영광의 순간을 서두르지 않습니다.

"그래서 부인은 재료들의 양을 평소대로 쟀죠. 그리고 그것들을 평소대로 섞었어요. 하지만 그럼에도 불구하고 평소와 다른 일이 생겼습니다. 왜 그런지 알려드려도 될까요?"

맥그래디 부인이 미소 지었습니다. "제발 그래주렴."

"왜냐하면 실수로 한 가지 추가 재료를 넣었기 때문이죠."

page 57

"내가?"

버스터는 고개를 끄덕였습니다. 그는 브라우니를 들어 그것을 두 개로 쪼갰습니다.

25센트 하나가 떨어졌습니다.

"오, 이런." 맥그래디 부인이 말했습니다. "어떻게 된 일이지?"

"아서 때문이에요." 버스터가 설명했습니다. "그가 들어왔을 때 부인은 통화 중이었어요. 그는 부인이 자기를 봤다고 생각했지만, 부인은 그러지 않았죠. 그리고 그는 동전이 든 가방을 다른 재료들 옆에 놓았어요. 그는 심지어 밀가루 약간을 그 가방 안에 쏟기까지 했었어요. 그게 아마도 부인이 알아차리지 못한 이유이죠."

맥그래디 부인은 다른 브라우니를 쪼갰고, 두 개의 25센트 동전이 떨어졌습니다.

"이제야 우리가 진실을 알았군." 하니 선생님이 말했습니다.

"아서는 결백해요!" 버스터가 외쳤습니다. "그를 풀어줄 시간이에요."

10장

page 58

어떤 종류의 탐정은 한 사건이 해결되면 어둠 속으로 사라져. 그 탐정에게는 미스터리를 푸는 것 자체가 그의 보상이야. 그는 텔레비전 카메라의 밝은 빛이나 신문의 첫 페이지를 이리저리 피하지.

다른 종류의 탐정은 좋은 일을 한 것에 대해 인정받고 칭찬받는 것을 좋아해. 그는 그가 마땅히 받아야 할 칭찬을 회피하지 않아. 나는 양쪽을 다 볼 수 있어. 그리고 어떤 탐정들이 사건을 해결한 것에 대해 공을 인정받는 걸 부끄러워하는 것을 이해해.

하지만 나는 그런 탐정이 아니야.

page 59

아서는 구금되어서 홀로 그의 생각과 함께 앉아 있었습니다. 그리고 바로 그 순간에는, 그의 생각은 그리 좋은 동행이 아니었습니다. 동전들은 없어졌고, 그의 명성은 도마에 올라 있었습니다. 만약에 언젠가 그가 결백하다는 것이 증명되어도, 그는 여전히 3학년 소풍을 놓치게 될 것이었습니다.

그는 옆방에서 팅글리 씨가 타자를 치는 소리를 들을 수 있었습니다. 키보드의 딸깍거리는 소리는 아서로 하여금 귀뚜라미가 우는 것을 떠오르게 했습니다. 적어도 귀뚜라미는 자신들이 원하는 일을 하는 데에 자유로웠습니다. 그들은 동전이나 소풍 혹은 예상치 못한 미스터리에 대해 걱정할 필요가 없었습니다.

갑자기 아서는 다른 소리를 들었습니다. 이것은 전혀 귀뚜라미처럼 들리지 않았습니다. 그것은 많은 사람들이 움직이는 소리처럼 들렸습니다.

팅글리 씨도 그 소리를 들었습니다. 그녀는 타자를 치는 것을 멈추고 이 소동이 무엇 때문인지 알아보려 일어났습니다.

page 60

그것은 많은 사람들이었습니다. 3학년 전체가 복도를 따라 오고 있었습니다. 학생들, 선생님들, 그리고 심지어 버스 운전사까지 거기에 있었습니다.

"무슨 일이에요?" 팅글리 씨가 물었습니다.

"뒤로 물러나세요." 하니 선생님이 그녀에게 충고했습니다. 그는 아서가 앉아 있던 방문을 열었습니다. "정의가 실현되려고 하고 있어요."

"아서, 내가 해냈어!" 버스터가 외쳤습니다. "넌 자유야!"

아서가 일어났습니다.

"내가? 하지만 어떻게?"

"우리가 없어진 동전에 대한 미스터리를 풀었단다." 하니 선생님이 설명했습니다. "그것들은 결국 맥그래디 부인의 브라우니에서 나타났어."

"정말요?" 아서가 말했습니다. 그는 그를 향해 미소 짓고 있는 랫번 선생님을 보았습니다.

"그건 아마도 부인이 만든 가장 비싼 브라우니일 거야." 브레인이 말했습니다.

모두들 웃었습니다.

"그리고," 버스터가 말했습니다. "넌 이 모든 것을 그 훌륭한 탐정에게 신세

진 거야. 그 비할 데 없는 수사관—"

page 61

버스터의 말은 하니 선생님이 확성기에 대고 말하는 바람에 중단되었습니다.

"버스로 돌아가요, 모두들!" 교장 선생님이 명령했습니다. "소풍이 기다리고 있어요!"

아이들이 밖으로 나가자, 아서는 버스터와 악수했습니다.

"고마워, 버스터. 난 거의 할 말을 잃었어. 넌 내가 아는 최고의 탐정이야!"

"난 네가 아는 유일한 탐정이잖아."

"뭐, 맞아. 하지만 여전히 네가 최고야."

"네가 그렇게 말한다면야."

"그래."

"좋아."

그는 버스를 타러 나가는 동안 내내 계속 그렇게 말했어. 나는 그를 멈추려고 하지 않았어. 좋은 탐정은 언제 뒤로 편안히 기대어 앉아 들어야 하는지 알기 때문이지.

소풍은 매우 성공적이었어. 이후에, 비록, 맥그래디 부인이 옆에 놓아둔 쿠키 접시가 갑자기 사라지는 새로운 미스터리를 직면하긴 했지만 말이야.

page 63

나는 내 셔츠에 붙은 부스러기들을

털어내고 막 시작하려고 하는 야구 게임에 합류했어. 만약 맥그래디 부인이 그 미스터리를 풀기를 원한다면, 그녀는 그걸 혼자 힘으로 해야만 할 거야.

Chapter 1

1. B *Hello, stranger. I'm Buster Baxter, private eye. You can call me Buster for short. I'm going to tell you about my first case. It involved my pal Arthur, some missing quarters, and a whole lot of trouble.*

2. A "I'm collecting money for Mrs. MacGrady's fund drive. We're going to buy a puppy for the fire department." He showed Binky a picture.

3. C "Don't tell anybody I gave. It's bad for my image."

4. B "This hat is not goofy," said Buster. It's a fedora –part of my new detective kit. I've been snooping—ah, looking for crimes."

5. D Buster leaned forward. "Third-grade picnic this Friday," he whispered.

Chapter 2

1. A Arthur hurried to the cafeteria kitchen.

2. D He could tell that Mr. Morris, the janitor, had cleaned the floors since lunch. "Clean enough to eat off of," Mr. Morris liked to say, but Arthur preferred plates.

3. B Mrs. MacGrady was on the phone.

4. C The bag was getting heavy in Arthur's hand. He went to put it down and accidentally knocked over the bag of flour.

5. B Arthur couldn't wait any longer. If he did, Buster would have a fit. Mrs. MacGrady was bound to be off the phone soon.

Chapter 3

1. B *When Arthur and I arrived at the arcade, I had two things on my mind. One was the games themselves. I wanted a return match with* Alien Explorer, *which had roughed me up the last time. That game needed to be taught a lesson. And I was just the one to do it. The other thing on my mind was finding a mystery to solve.*

2. C "Buster," said Arthur, "what are you doing with that magnifying glass?"

3. A Buster looked closer. "Definitely some kind of powder." Arthur looked down. There was a little . . . Suddenly he smiled. "Oh, that's no mystery. When

1 was dropping off the quarters in the cafeteria, I accidentally spilled some flour. It must have gotten on my shirt."

4. D Buster was out of money, but Arthur still had enough for one more game. He decided to try a pinball machine.

5. A When they left the arcade, Buster was still excited. "My best friend hit the high score," he said proudly to one and all.

Chapter 4

1. A *As much as I hated to admit it, I was starting to feel a little down. Why was it so hard to find a mystery to investigate?*

2. B As they passed the principal's office, Mr. Haney waved them in. "Good morning, Arthur, Buster," he said. "Oh, Arthur, don't forget to give Mrs. MacGrady the quarters you collected for her fund drive."

3. D "You were responsible for them. If that money doesn't turn up, I'm afraid you'll have to serve a day—" . . . "I mean, a week of after-school detention." Mr. Haney paused. "And no third grade picnic for you tomorrow."

4. C "No problem! I could solve this case in my sleep. Well, no, I guess I'd have to be awake. And not wearing my pajamas, either. But don't worry, Arthur. Buster Baxter is on the case. You'll be going to that picnic tomorrow. Trust me."

5. B "Try not to get me into any deeper trouble than I'm in now. Things are bad enough as it is."

Chapter 5

1. D *In every case there's a key witness, and this case was no different. I knew who she was, and she knew who she was, too. Last name: MacGrady.*

2. B "Maybe you should talk to Mr. Morris," Mrs. MacGrady suggested.

3. C "Changing a lightbulb. Then I got the call to go to the kitchen. Seems Mrs. MacGrady was having some trouble with her mixer. When I got there, the floor was covered with brownie batter. So I cleaned up the mess."

4. C "Just a minute, Mr. Morris." Buster ran to catch up to him. "That jingling"

. . . It sounds like quarters. *A lot of quarters!*" Mr. Morris pulled a huge key ring full of keys from his pocket. "I know what you mean," he said, jingling it. I've often thought the same thing myself."

5. B It wasn't really all right, thought Buster, at least not for Arthur. He had hoped to get to the bottom of the case quickly. But the more he dug, the more complicated the case became.

Chapter 6

1. B *I thought maybe a change of scene would help, so I made my way to the suspect's home. There I met up with the suspect's sister. She seemed to be a pretty cool customer but I knew I could handle her.*

2. A "Ready? Okay, take this down. Every single word." Buster nodded. "THAT . . . HAT . . . LOOKS . . . SILLY . . . ON . . . YOU." Buster put down his pencil. "This is serious, D.W. Besides, I like the hat."

3. C "He wouldn't just bring the money into the house. Too many questions to answer. Too many people might see it. But he'd want it close by. Hidden. Safe. But where? That's what I can't quite figure out. Not that Arthur's so clever. But still . . ."

4. D "Of course!" she shouted. "*We* should check the lawn for signs of recent digging."

5. C Arthur stared at D.W. and started to say something, but Buster held up his hand. "You're better off not asking," he said. "You really don't want to know."

Chapter 7

1. C *Could he really be a criminal mastermind? I tried to picture him in his secret hideout swimming in a sea of shiny quarters. They dripped through his fingers as he laughed insanely. Quarters! Quarters! He could never get enough.*

2. C "But you've only had two helpings of dessert. That's not like you, Buster. You're sure you don't have a headache or fever?" Buster shook his head. "It's

just this case, Mom. I haven't figured out how to help Arthur yet."

3. A "You're a good friend, Buster. I'm sure Arthur appreciates that."

4. D "Really?" Arthur got all excited. "So, tell me." "Okay. Well, the quarters were stolen by an army of evil robots. They need the metal for fuel. Nobody noticed them because they can transform themselves into . . . into . . . any shape."

5. B "You'd better get some sleep," said Arthur. "Okay," said Buster. "You too."

Chapter 8

1. D *Detectives are supposed to be tough, but even they feel the pain when a friend is hurting.*

2. A "People might begin to think you're my partner in crime. You could be my accomplice, my henchman, my—"

3. B "Forget it," said Arthur. "You did your best. You might be a lousy detective—" "*Bad*, Arthur. I said *bad*."

4. C "Sorry about this, Arthur." "Me, too, Mr. Ratburn." His teacher nodded. "Don't give up. I'm sure the truth will come out in the end."

5. D "I know how you feel," said the Brain. "Sometimes when I'm working on a tough math problem, I feel like my brain's overflowing with data." "Keep it moving," said Mr. Haney. Buster stepped onto the bus. Suddenly he stopped and stared at the Brain. "Overflowing? Overflowing!"

Chapter 9

1. B *Every detective wants to be cool, calm, and collected at all times.*

2. D "Mrs. MacGrady, do you know why your brownie mix overflowed?" "Not really. I don't mind saying it was a little embarrassing. But Mr. Morris was very nice about helping me clean it up." "Has that ever happened before? The overflowing, I mean." "No. I'm always very careful. But this time I guess I made too much." "Did you use a different recipe?" Mrs. MacGrady stopped to

think. "Well, no, now that you mention it. The recipe was the same as always." "Did you use any new equipment?"

3. C   Buster was getting to it. But detectives never rush their moments of glory.

4. A   Buster nodded. He picked up the brownie and broke it in two. A quarter fell out.

5. B   "It was Arthur," Buster explained. "You were on the phone when he came in. He thought you saw him, but you didn't. Then he left the bag of quarters next to the other ingredients. He had even spilled some of your flour on his bag, which is probably why you didn't notice."

Chapter 10

1. D   *I could see both sides, and I understood that some detectives would be shy about taking credit for untangling things. But I wasn't one of them.*

2. A   Arthur was sitting in detention alone with his thoughts.

3. C   He could hear Miss Tingley typing in the next room. The clicking on the keyboard made Arthur think of crickets chirping.

4. B   "They must be the richest brownies she's ever made," said the Brain. Everyone laughed.

5. C   *I brushed a few crumbs off my shirt and joined in the baseball game that was starting up. If Mrs. MacGrady wanted to solve that mystery, she was going to have to do it on her own.*

아서, 도둑으로 몰리다!
(Arthur Accused!)

1판 1쇄   2013년 9월 2일
2판 1쇄   2024년 4월 22일

지은이   Marc Brown
기획   김승규
책임편집   김보경 차소향
콘텐츠제작및감수   롱테일 교육 연구소
저작권   명채린
마케팅   두잉글 사업 본부

펴낸이   이수영
펴낸곳   롱테일북스
출판등록   제2015-000191호
주소   04033 서울특별시 마포구 양화로 113, 3층(서교동, 순흥빌딩)
전자메일   help@ltinc.net

ISBN 979-11-91343-63-2 14740